THE BEST BOSS

HOW TO BECOME A GREAT MANAGER WITH LEADERSHIP SKILLS AND STRATEGIES TO GUIDE TEAMS

MICHAEL HOFFMAN

CONTENTS

INTRODUCTION

But what makes a great leader today? Someone who is an all-knowing superhero? Someone who commands others what to do? Or someone who should be feared and cannot be disobeyed? That's the old image and impression of what leadership was and should have been like. What's also outdated are the leadership programs that continue to train you for a world that *was,* not for a world of the future, but a world that is becoming increasingly globalised and diversified. A world where borders and the lines that divide us are slowly disappearing as technology connects employees and teams around the world. Teams today consists of a wide range of talent, from employees who work on-premise to employees who work remotely. Members of the same team could even be working in a different country or continent altogether.

> "It is one thing to be a boss, another thing to be a mentor, but a completely different thing to be a leader." ~ Unknown

It's common to struggle with being in a position of authority and not knowing what to do. For many people, the idea of leadership and being a boss throws up complex emotions. Even if you are a worker, trying to understand what kind of behavior should be acceptable within an organization can seem difficult. We all struggle while trying to understand how to organize our homes, society, and workplaces.

This book focuses on the role of the boss. The aim is to study what being a boss means traditionally in business organizations and how the meaning of the term is evolving along with new-age styles of doing business. It is undeniable that all infrastructures need a boss; people have to be guided and told what to do; otherwise, there can be mayhem. Yet, what it means to be a boss has changed over the years, and people have become less tolerant of bad bosses who treat their employees without respect and dignity. Gone are the days of strict hierarchies where whatever the boss says goes.

The purpose of this book is to show you how being a boss isn't about being on top belting out orders, but being part of the team and connecting with the employees. Organizational structures in the modern era require democratic spaces; employees want their bosses to be approachable and their feelings to be validated rather than shut down.

My name is Michael Hoffman, and I have been working with Star-tups and Big Business alike for close to two decades now, and in this time I have noticed some things about management tactics - what works and what doesn't. More than anything else, I have learned that people just want to feel validated and worthy. This makes a lot of sense; in a way, it's very similar to the relationship I have with my daughter or my wife. At the end of the day, we are all just human beings, and we want to relate to each other as such, as equals.

I have noticed an increasing rise in this trend because of the genera-tional shift within the workforce. Hence, I implore you, as a new leader to evolve with the times. After spending the past six years working for a top-notch marketing agency out of the US, where I managed five different generations of workers at once, I felt compelled to share some of this valuable insight. This book is my hope to help you bypass the mistakes I have made so you can step boldly into your role as a boss and leader.

The ultimate goal is to teach you how to become such a good boss that your workforce doesn't even recognize you as one anymore. The perfect leader is one who can shed any social performance of authority to assimilate within the larger mass of workers, while at the same time retaining professional credibility in the eyes of the employees. Your employees should come to you for help, as they would go to a friend for advice. This book will teach you how you can achieve this and how it will benefit your organization.

Once employees start to feel like they can speak up, they will come up with innovative ideas, find ways to increase the efficiency of the organization while working harder to produce better results. All you need is for your employees to trust you, like you, and see you as the ideal role model. The core behind the success of any organization is employee satisfaction; if your workers like what they do, they will do it, not just for the money but for the personal value they derive from it too.

There is no replacing a dedicated and personalized workforce who believe in the vision and purpose of the organization. Most workspaces are saddled with employees who would rather be away from work – most workers just want to get done with work and go home. But, a loyal workforce will stay behind to complete the job and ensure that consistent quality is maintained to further help the business thrive.

An example of democratic leadership that helps each individual and, consequently, the whole team is jazz. This might seem like a strange place to look for leadership lessons, but there's a lot you can learn from jazz bands. A typical jazz ensemble consists of ten musicians with each playing a different instrument. A jazz band has one single leader whose responsibility is to direct each individual to create a cohesive production.

While the coordinator technically controls each musician, what makes jazz truly democratic is that within the structure of the sheet music, at specific moments, each musician is given the freedom to innovate and show off his creativity. Just like a good leader allows his employees to express their thoughts and ideas.

With the expert tricks and tips in this book, you'll be able to learn what good leadership looks like, allowing you to become the best boss there is. In a competitive space, new leadership skills help organizations to enhance their profitability. So, if you want a leg up on your competition, whether it's another company or a coworker fighting for the same promotion, this book will teach you the truth behind great leadership paving the road for your success.

The knowledge you are about to access comes from years of experience and is proven to work. Business is constantly changing in our fast-paced world, and if you want to stay on top, you have to adapt to these changes. This book will guide you by detailing why the old methods are redundant and what the characteristics are of being a great boss in this new age of doing business.

CHAPTER 1
THE KEY DIFFERENCE BETWEEN A BOSS AND A LEADER

The term 'boss' highlights a position of authority, someone who is in charge of a place or an organization. Everywhere you go, someone is telling you what to do, where to be, and how to behave, this rule enforcer is generally regarded as a boss. In our daily life, when someone tries to control us in this way, we tend to challenge their authority because we like to retain our ability to choose. Yet, when we walk into the workplace, our brain forgets this, and we accept the system of hierarchy which the workplace organization is based on.

Being 'bossy' has now become synonymous with being dictatorial, shutting people down, and directing them without listening to what they want. Everyone has a horrific story of being treated badly by their boss and not being able to do anything about it. The problem with this term is that it's vague – it doesn't highlight any important quality that a boss should possess. Neither does it tell you what makes a good boss and a bad boss. This vagueness and the subsequent assumption of the superiority of any boss, regardless of their behavior, is the starting point for all workplace problems.

What we need is some direction amid all this confusion. The term *boss* is outdated because it doesn't tell us what a good boss or a bad boss is – it just tells us to follow the whims of a person just because they have the title of being boss.

Let's dive deep into this terminology to deconstruct what it means to be a 'boss.' What is the boss? The term boss is defined in opposition to the number of people that exist below this position – a boss is an individual who is the immediate supervisor of a certain amount of employees who are required to take orders and submit their work for the approval. In most cases, it's not a formal title as much as it is a colloquial term used to refer to anybody who exists in a position of authority higher than the average employee, and hence, includes supervisors, managers, and CEOs.

The role of the boss exists to organize the workplace. The assumption behind this is the belief that people can't manage their work and must be directed to bring out the best in them. It seems to most people that without a boss, the workspace will fall into anarchy. This is why a workplace has managers who direct the work of those below them. It is commonly expected that a boss will ensure the tasks and goals set by the company are met in the stipulated amount of time.

It might seem like the position of being a boss is full of privilege with no taxation, but that's a lie. At the end of the day, if the work isn't done, the boss is always held accountable. If there is any problem within the organization, it impacts the boss's peace of mind. While an individual employee needs to be concerned only with his work, the boss must be concerned with everyone's work. If anyone is not pulling their weight, it's the boss who has to put in the extra effort to get the job done. The boss is accountable to the organization as a whole while the employee is just accountable for his one or two tasks.

PROS AND CONS OF BEING A BOSS

In this section, we're going to take a look at the advantages and disadvantages that come with being a boss. This will help us to arrive at a balanced viewpoint about the position of being a boss.

Being a boss means having complete control over what you do. As opposed to being the person who gets told what to do, you get to decide what is to be done. This freedom of choice is an exclusive commodity that only a boss is allowed to wield.

If you're a good boss, you will generate loyalty in your subordinates who will be willing to do anything to complete the task you have set for them. It's hard to deny that as a boss, you depend on others to fulfill their jobs and duties – this is why you need a loyal workforce that is willing to listen to you.

As a boss, there are always people who are more than willing to help you finish the tasks you have to get done. The boss is the center of a collaborative effort and, in that sense, technically receives the most help from other people.

When the work doesn't get done, you're the one who is held accountable. The employees will simply go home because the result doesn't impact them. You're the one who has to serve up the end product, and when it's not up to the mark, it's your problem and not that of the workers. Employees don't botter anything beyond their work because that's all they are required to care about.

Being a boss can be a daunting experience because everyone expects you always to know what to do. Whenever there is a crisis, it's the boss who everyone turns to; you're the one who has to think quickly and come up with innovative solutions to resolve the situation. While the workers are required to put in their labor, you're required to think, and that can itself be taxing because one wrong idea can lead to huge problems for the whole organization.

Once an employee has finished what they have to do, they go home. But the boss has to stay until the end, compiling and reviewing everyone else's work. It's down to them to pick up the slack and make sure everything is done correctly, with no excuses.

Being a boss has multiple dimensions to it; it can be rewarding when the work gets done on time and flawlessly, but you also receive the scorn of the employees because, for them, you are the one forcing them to waste their life working.

SO, WHAT MAKES A BAD BOSS?

Demanding: Employees are people too and not productivity machines who should get the work done no matter what. When you demand too much from people, they get burnt out, and the whole workplace suffers. As a boss, you can't have unrealistic expectations about the amount of work an employee can get done. To expect an employee to do the task of ten others is going to make you a bad boss because the person doing the work knows that too much is being asked of them. They will stop giving their best to the work they do and just finish things without caring about the quality.

Judgmental: A bad boss is one that makes people feel uncomfortable, guilty, or ashamed. Most people think that when they shame and judge people, it will incentivize them to work harder. This might work for some employees, but for many, this becomes a reason to start hating their work. You can't push people to work harder. You have to hold their hands along the way to allow their creativity and productivity to flourish.

When you judge others, you are automatically putting your own opinions and belief over that of someone else. This hinders the process of empathy creation because you aren't opening yourself up to the experience of others. As a boss, you must remember that you come from a certain place and time, which means that your opinions and values will differ from that of your employees. That's why it's your task to be non-judgmental toward others. What you might think is wrong or strange, might be perfectly acceptable for someone else.

This doesn't mean that you leave your critical thinking aside – just keep an open mind and consider everything, instead of dismissing it on face value. There are times when, as a boss, your feelings will be in direct disagreement with the feelings of others, but you have to ensure that you don't let this disagreement factor into your judgment. In many ways, as a boss, you have to understand the reason that drove someone to do something, rather than simply being angry and dismissive of the person for doing it.

. . .

Belittling/Condescending: When people are in positions of power, they tend to see those below them as sub-human entities who don't deserve respect, only condescension. This adds to the toxic environment of a workplace because employees start to feel like they can't trust their boss and, instead, start seeing the boss as someone to be scared of. Leading to a lack of communication because there is very little trust between the boss and the worker. When an employee isn't able to do something, they are far more likely to hide it than come to you for help. At the end of the day, this bodes badly for the organization because the work did not get done.

Non-Approachable: As a boss, you have to let go of your ego and see the world from your subordinates' perspectives. You can't motivate people without empathizing with them and understanding them. A person's ability to carry out work and produce labor is dependent on many factors, and without being entirely aware of what's going on in their life, you can't understand how to make him or her focus on a project. You have to be an approachable figure who people can reach out to with their problems. This way, you can know what's going on with your employees and why they aren't able to perform their best.

Controlling: You can't control your employees, and you have to accept that. All you can do is *tell them* what to do, give them the means to do it, and hope that they succeed. If you try to dictate what your employees should do all the time, it can lead to frustration, anger, and demotivation. When you let them do what they wish to do, employees start to feel like they have your trust. The best motivator for most people is to allow them to challenge themselves. If you showcase your confidence in their abilities and leave them alone, they're far more likely to push themselves to prove they deserve your trust.

WHAT MAKES A GOOD BOSS?

Leadership: Well, a good boss isn't a boss at all but is more of a leader. Leadership is an action, as opposed to a position of authority. It's making yourself invisible and sparse as you direct the work of your employees and the organization. Leadership isn't about putting your-self in the forefront, but handling things from the background. This inherently makes the act of leading a less dictatorial form of organiza-tion than being a boss.

What is a leader? It is not about management because, unlike a manager, a leader doesn't direct. Instead, a leader promotes self-accountability – this changes how the relationship between the upper echelon and the employees work. Instead of it being a hierarchal rela-tionship, it becomes one of equality, whereby the worker isn't account-able to the leader. The worker is solely responsible only to themselves for their work. A manager controls every aspect of what an employee does, but a leader simply builds confidence and encourages employees rather than supervising every aspect of work.

Leadership, most importantly, isn't a title or pay grade that sepa-rates you from the masses of workers. Being a leader is about changing your outlook and vision toward work. You are as much a worker as the person making the product your company sells, the only difference you should look at is that you motivate and direct the workforce, while the other person does the work. A leader is simply a person of social influence whose words matter to employees because they have exper-tise in how things should be done. An employee isn't required to listen to a leader but does so because it helps them to do their work better and motivates them.

What makes a good leader? A great leader isn't academic and forceful but believes in a two-way communication where the voice and input of the employee are valued. Leadership is about communication, not enforcing orders that must be fulfilled – this makes the workspace a far more democratic space where the leader isn't an overarching figure of authority that must be listened to. Instead, he or she becomes a mentor and a friend who clarifies and communicates the tasks effec-tively to be done.

THE QUALITIES OF A STRONG LEADER

Clarity: When employees don't know what to do exactly, they tend to fail at their work. Clarity doesn't just involve making it clear to employees what the task of the day is, but is equally about being clear about the overall goals and objectives of the workplace. Your employees need to know what the larger goal is that they are working toward – what's the purpose of the organization they are working for.

As a strong leader, you have to make a person see the larger picture, so they get motivated to work harder, which only comes with a sense of purpose. As an example, there was an organization that took old electronic components and converted them into usable products. These components were about to be thrown out; they would have contributed to environmental degradation and, by making them into something else, the organization gave their employees a reason to care about their work, to feel as though they were making a positive change in the world.

Clarity of thought leads to a streamlined work process. Your employees should know what the destination is and the steps they have to take to get there.

Opportunity: A strong leader makes work more interesting by turning it into a game of opportunities. People work because it allows them to grow and become better. A workspace that offers no new opportunities ends up becoming a boring one that loses all interest. You should give your employees new tasks that fall outside of their comfort zone, so they get new opportunities to learn valuable skills. This way, your employees will be interested in the work they are doing; they will learn new skills they can apply to their work, bringing in newfound innovation to the workplace, and the overall team satisfaction will also rise.

The development of employees is key to the development of the whole organization. The more that people are challenged, the more incentivized they are to perform better.

· · ·

Involvement: If you force people to do work they don't feel personally connected to, it will seem like a task to them. When we are interested in what we are doing, it stops seeming like work to us, and doing labor becomes easier. You can't expect your workers to be alienated from the decision-making process and yet, still perform wonderfully. Only when they feel like they are part of the team and their input matters, will the employees personally connect themselves to the work they are supposed to do.

You should encourage individuals to work with you when you're planning the project. When people are put in positions of power, they automatically assume they have a responsibility to do better and start to feel a sense of accountability toward the company. This makes them care about the work and its successful completion. So, make sure that your employees are required to think about decision making so that they feel part of the process.

This also benefits the organization in general because it clarifies communication and ensures job satisfaction. This way, everyone knows what they have to do. It familiarizes the employees with the organizational structure of the company. You should also acknowledge and appreciate your employees' ideas because it will give them the push they need to continue improving and innovating their working style. They will come up with faster ways to complete tasks, and this will make them feel like their voice matters.

When involving your employees in the decision-making process, make sure you don't defer your complete authority to them. You should make them feel like their input is welcome but retain the final decision-making power.

Keep Commitments: A leader is only valuable if they are trustable. If you don't keep the commitments you make to your employees, they will quickly lose any kind of trust they had in you. A leader who can't stand up to his words does not inspire loyalty. Your employees will have no reason to believe in the vision you have set in front of them. As a leader, you must remember that your employees are also taking a risk when they believe in your vision and start working toward its successful completion.

Consistency: All organizations want to be consistent; take the example of fast-food chains. They encourage loyalty in their customers only because they promise to keep the quality of the food consistent across state and international boundaries. So, when you walk into one of them anywhere in the world, you expect the same quality of food to be served to you, and that is what makes you loyal to a brand.

As a leader, you have to replicate this kind of consistency by ensuring that the values and goals of the organization don't fluctuate from day-to-day. All employees need a level of familiarity to guide them, and knowing that there is a consistent standard of work they are expected to produce will keep them satisfied. All they want is the great work they did yesterday to be still considered suitable for the rest of the year.

If a leader praises one person for the same work while reprimanding another, it's going to create stress and nervousness among the employees because they will start to think there is a system in place. This also means that as a leader, you must treat everyone equally and not show any signs of favoritism.

Respect: It's astounding how badly some leaders treat their employees and how blind they are to the negative impact this has on the overall growth of the organization. When people feel like someone is abusing their position of power to put them down, they start to hate the entire structure of the organization itself, which is clearly not a good motivator.

All you need to respect people is to hear what they are saying and understand where they are coming from. A leader should not be the center of an organization and should not see themselves as such. Your purpose should only be to treat your employees kindly, so they feel inspired to work.

No leader can achieve anything without the people who believe in him or her. If you are leading a team, you must be appreciative of their talents and support. As an inspiring leader, you must avoid taking all the credit and learn to be humble. When you acknowledge employees for their priceless efforts, you will be appreciated and respected. People would never like a leader who takes credit for their work and criticizes their efforts.

If you constantly put your team down, they will feel like they do not have a purpose. The employees need to feel the opposite if they ever want to be inspired by you. Learn to thank them while encouraging them to work through their insecurities. Remind the people who support you that they are worthy of great things in life. Reassure them of the value they bring to your cause.

Praise: Many leaders use praise sparingly, not realizing the immense power they have in their hands to motivate their employees. Most people don't believe in themselves, and they need external validation to make them feel like they matter. Many workers crave such validation from figures of power and authority whose word matters far more in their eyes than their own. By appreciating and rewarding people, you will create an incentive system that will push people to work harder.

This is why you should reward excellent and exceptional work with tokens of appreciation, such as medals, certifications, or even perks. When you do give such memorabilia, remember to mention the specific act, their name, and everything else that personalizes the achievement for them. They should feel seen and heard; also, make sure that you don't just distribute such things to everyone because it has to be a rare commodity to make people work for it.

If you think this might be too much for your organization, even a heartfelt "thank you" or "good job" can make people feel like what they are doing is meaningful.

BOSS VS. LEADER

Both concepts of being a leader and a boss assume that on some level, employees need a guiding hand that has to direct their work and give them tasks to do. The difference arises in the outlook generated by these two words – a leader is part of the team, while a boss stands above the unit. Being a boss is about being controlling and authoritative because the use of the word itself carries connotations of superiority. The problem with this is that once supervisors and managers start seeing themselves as "bosses," they automatically start thinking that a hierarchical system based on dominance and dictatorship is the best way to organize a company. As we have discussed above, this leads to multiple problems for the organization and creates a toxic environment.

Being a leader, on the other hand, is about guiding people not by shouting at them or just giving orders, but by being inclusive and a member of the team. A leader isn't separate from the crowd, but someone who works with the group, taking care to treat everyone equally, being respectful, and getting the maximum productivity out of people by motivating and inspiring them. A leader isn't just concerned with the work being done, but how it's being done and if the employees are happy while doing the work.

Bosses tend to be judgmental and only see the world from their perspective, unwilling to listen to what anyone else has to say. This lack of empathy in bosses is a result of their self-assumed superiority that makes them think their rationality and judgment is the only important one in the room. However, being a leader is about getting rid of such assumptions and learning to empathize with other people's situations and perspectives. This exercise of building understanding with the employees leads to the creation of strong communication bonds within the organization that inspires people to work harder.

Many bosses just hark orders at people – a leader listens to what other people have to say, encourages others to speak up, allowing those who generally keep their mouths shut, due to intimidation, to approach their superiors with problems and concerns. When the whole organization works with this attitude of approachability and clear communication, work gets done faster, and the quality of the work is guaranteed to be good.

A boss is never able to get people to work harder and only ends up cultivating employee dissatisfaction that hampers the effectiveness and efficiency of the work process. A leader allows people to get invested in their work, making work seem like play. Fear is a bad motivator to push people to care about their work. When employees feel like their inputs are valued, and they are a respected member of the organization, they not only finish their work in time, but also work harder to ensure the overall prosperity of the organization. Only a leader can cultivate such a positive attitude and not a boss, as we will discuss in the next chapter.

WHY THE BEST BOSS ISN'T ONE

If you change your perception about what it means to be a boss, being a boss and a leader is kind of the same thing. When we start seeing it as a role of care and empathy, rather than one of dominance, we've achieved the goal of being a better manager. So, the distinction between the two terms is only a semantic one. But, for the purpose of this book, we have to distinguish between a boss and a leader to highlight two different approaches toward the management of employees. As stated in the last chapter, being a boss means following a traditional model of organization that is based on bossing employees around, while being a leader is about seeing yourself on the same plane as your employees.

This distinction is key to understanding the modern form of doing business. Business is changing rapidly, and you have to adapt to the changes not only in the consumer market but also in relation to employee expectations. New graduates have a different approach toward work – they don't believe that work is worship, and they must give everything to it. They expect their workplace to care about them and give back as much as they are providing. This is why people want leadership these days and not tyrannical bosses.

Many companies have even gotten rid of management completely in new overhauls as a way to democratize the working space. But, these kinds of strategies don't work in the long run because it leads to a chaotic environment that is not conducive for a healthy work environment. People still want some sort of direction; they don't want leadership to vanish entirely – they just want to be led and not bossed around.

This is why you have to be a leader in the contemporary working space – you have to be a humble person who is down to earth, cares about his employees, is willing to listen to his employees, and is ready to set his ego aside for the betterment of the company. This doesn't mean you should just start relinquishing all power and control; instead, you need to find a balance between seeming like a powerful and determined figure and maintaining your approachability.

Managers who don't understand other people and what they are feeling don't know if they're being heard. Without being able to read and understand other people's positions, all you're doing is shouting orders at them without even thinking if they have acknowledged them and will be able to fulfill them. A leader listens to his employees and their problems to ensure that they can do their work on time. This makes communication more fruitful, and instead of blaming the employee when they aren't able to finish the task on time, you can ensure that they do finish their work because you put yourself in their shoes and helped them solve their problems.

CHAPTER 2
CHANGING TIMES

Times have changed and will continue to do so. It's not the older generation that determines business practices and values now, but the newer one. The new generation knows what their rights are and are far more sensitive to criticism. They don't want a work environment that thrives on competition and exploitation – they want one that is empathetic and caring. As times will continue to change at a rapid pace, you have to adjust your organizational structure and method to account for how work is done contemporarily.

Managers are the reason for many people leaving their jobs. The most attractive quality of companies these days is how they treat their employees. In the world of social media, every small thing you do will be publicized, so you have to maintain your reputation and keep it flawless. Management style impacts the mood of employees, which determines how they feel about their work, and that in turn determines if they will give everything they have to their work that day or not. Most employees don't want to go to work because they hate their workplace environment and not the job itself. An exciting workplace where the manager acts as your friend can be a massive boost to the morale and motivation of the whole team.

Today's youth wants autonomy over their work and the choices they make. They don't want a surveillance officer in the form of a manager who is watching everything they do. They want freedom outside the workplace and within it as well. As a manager, you have to concede to this demand, but that doesn't mean you can't still lead them. Just because they don't wish to be bossed around doesn't mean they don't want direction. As a manager, you have to change your approach to seem more like a part of the team. Encourage innovation, collaboration, and respect your employees – this way, they will want to be led, rather than you forcing them to listen to you.

BEING BOSSY IS DETRIMENTAL

Being bossy isn't just an awful attitude; it's a bad business approach – it hurts your team and their productivity.

When you take on a bossy attitude and approach, you become unwilling to learn from your employees. This collapses the space of collaboration and communication that is the key to innovation. New information and ideas come from the people working on the ground level who are experiencing how the work is being done. They can point out the flaws in the supply chain or the places where costs can be cut to boost profits. Bosses tend to shut down such innovative thinking because it threatens their position. A leader, on the other hand, is assured of his intelligence and hence, empower others to flourish rather than shutting them down.

A true leader does not work alone. When you carefully listen to what people have to say, you show that you have faith in them. People are not inspired by others who trust their own vision alone. They want leaders who listen to the grievances of people carefully and make decisions democratically.

As a leader, you should invite people to present their opinions before you make crucial decisions. You have to remember that whatever you decide also affects the future of the people working with you. If you are running a company, make space for employees to access face-to-face interactions with you. Strengthen office interaction and encourage employees through an "open-door" policy. When people talk to you on a day-to-day basis, they will also learn to trust you.

Bossing people around automatically implies that you don't trust their judgment. At the very onset of the work process itself, you have created a work culture where employees don't trust themselves and look at you for guidance. But, at the same time, you expect them to do their job well, innovatively, and to use their judgment. This contradiction is harmful for the organization because it restricts the freedom of employees. Personal freedom allows people to invest some part of their individuality into the work process; when this independence is taken away, workers become disillusioned and frustrated. This also hampers the creativity required to make a company successful.

It's necessary to maintain only some amount of discipline among the employees because it ensures that they do not undermine the authority of their seniors and the managers who are supposed to overlook them. It's better to have a perfect combination of centralized and decentralized organizational structures. It ensures the employees can work without too many restrictions but are required to follow the rules and procedures of the organization. It is the perfect combination of discipline and freedom of action. This way, the employees can work freely to increase the level of work done in the organization while at the same time following a certain code of conduct.

People want to believe in their leaders and get inspired by them. But when leaders start acting like perfect Gods who know everything and are without flaws, it intimidates employees. Many people crave such intimidation because it ensures that everyone trusts their knowledge, and their opinion is always valued. This can be a good quality when exercised with restraint, but when it goes overboard, it makes employees scared of their leaders. It ends up making you seem like a know-it-all, which makes most workers believe that their opinions are prima facie wrong, and not worth even uttering. This leads to stagnation in communication because people will just expect you always to be right and will never share their ideas, opinions, or criticisms, which will hurt the organization.

A leader does not boost his expertise and shove it into people's faces. You should use your knowledge to push the creativity of your employee. Many employees have great ideas that just need honing – it's your task to guide, not to dictate.

FREEDOM

Human beings are inherently creative beings, and we like to make things and take pride in what we do. Since the Stone Age, people have been defined by the work they do, and it's one of the most important aspects of living a meaningful life. This connection with our work is broken when we are not allowed to do anything ourselves in the work we do. That is what makes labor a mindless job where you just sit and do things without caring about it. This can leave people feeling sad and disappointed; it makes them feel like their life has no meaning, and the work they are doing is drudgery.

A sense of freedom allows people to feel autonomous and in control. It will enable them to have a meaningful relationship with their work, as opposed to an exploitative one. As a leader, you should take time to understand your employees and what they expect out of their work. Work might mean a lack of freedom, but within that, as long as employees feel like their desires are being recognized and fulfilled, they will feel satisfied with their jobs.

Here's what you can do to encourage a sense of freedom in your employees:

Freedom is about the illusion of choice. While most employees don't get to do exactly what they want in life, within the workspace being allowed to choose when you work, how you work, and make small decisions, enables employees to relatively feel like they are free to do what they want. Decision making and having choices makes us feel like we're free because we have options. Consideration itself allows us to feel like we are in control of our lives, and you should let your employees choose whenever it's possible.

When people do a job where they are forced to do work they are not interested in or connected to, they feel burnt out and without any purpose. They feel like they have no control over their lives and are just mindlessly following someone else's orders. But, when employees get to work in a firm that allows them to do the work they want while at the same time allowing them to serve a cause that they perceive is bigger than themselves, they feel connected to the work they're doing. This ensures that your employees are happy and work without any resistance or push.

You should actively showcase your trust in your employees by allowing them to go through with projects without asking them to seek your approval for everything. You should change your approach toward supervision by having friendly chats as a way of keeping up with the progress of their work rather than forcing them to report to you formally.

Work has to be individualized. Everyone is inspired by the story of Mark Zuckerberg because, in him, we see how our uniqueness can contribute to creating important changes in the world. Freedom is all about being able to create things that come from the core of our individuality and subjectivity. Creative work makes employees feel invested – they take care to be perfect, leave no room for mistakes, and work overtime to get it done.

Without freedom, we aren't connected to the work we do. We just do what we're told without coming up with new ideas and without any energy or optimism to finish the project. Without freedom, people work like drones; they don't think carefully about what they're doing because they simply don't care. This kind of uncaring attitude is prevalent everywhere because employees don't feel like what they think is valued. In most cases, they are required to hide their uniqueness and conform to the work standards. When they feel like their individuality is respected and celebrated, they will come up with ideas and innovations that will revolutionize the workspace. So, remember to encourage your employees to contribute by caring about them rather than expecting them to follow orders mindlessly.

All employees want to be valued and understood. They want their problems to be taken up in the workspace, their struggles highlighted, and their work ethic rewarded. Employees usually look for their superiors to validate and appreciate them.

Understanding employees is all about individualizing them rather than seeing them as objects. Learn about people, refer to them with their names, and learn the names of their spouse, children, and even pets. Go to people's houses to see how they live outside of work and the troubles they have going on. All of this will make people more real to you, and less like objects that come to work to fulfill your commands. Smile when you are listening to somebody, also nod to show the responsiveness, and encourage people to speak up. If you have a negative viewpoint or the need to reprimand somebody, don't let it show and talk to them politely outside of work. Also, be genuine in your appreciation and praise for people.

When you lead people, your behavior and body language should communicate the respect you have for them and their work. It is not enough for you to send greeting cards and flowers when they are sick if you disrespect them daily. Cultivate a positive and appreciative working environment. Spend time with your employees if you are the boss - have office meetups and light-hearted breaks. Let the people know that they are valued as human beings above all else.

Stress ruins interpersonal equations and communication. When you are having a bad day, make sure you do not take it out on your employees. A strong leader should have constructive discussions in times of crisis. Remind your employees that their failures do not make them subject to taunts and trauma. Embolden them every day as a show of thanks for their past and future efforts. To succeed, you need the loyalty of the people you are leading. If people do not trust you, they are likely to go against your vision under challenging situations.

MICROMANAGING

As a leader, you have to know your boundaries with your employees. It's okay to want to check on what your workers are doing and the status of the project. It's another thing to be overbearing, breathing down their necks at every second and forcing them to waste their valuable time by regularly checking on their progress. Bosses tend to micromanage their employees when they think they know better, believing that without their expertise, nothing will be done right. This attitude can lead to a toxic environment where employees feel like they have to be on the watch constantly. You want your employees to be open with you, not guarded against you.

Many people normalize micromanaging, believing it be an essential aspect of being a boss. You can find out if you're micromanaging by checking how many times you tried to find fault with your employee's work only to find out that it turned out to be perfectly fine. This means that your employees were working correctly, yet you felt the need not to trust them and check on them. Micromanagers also tend to want reports and records for everything, which can drive subordinates crazy. If you think that every meeting needs to be perfectly recorded, all emails and phone calls to be logged in, you're a micromanager.

Micromanagers end up creating a work environment where employees stop holding themselves accountable. They expect you to check on them to see if the work is perfect or not, instead of reviewing it themselves. Since you can't possibly check up on them every day and ensure that every part of their work is up to the mark, it's going to end up hurting the organization's quality. You need to make your employees feel responsible for their work rather than being their supervisor. They should find problems and concerns and bring them to you rather than waiting for you to check on them.

Micromanagement also means that the leader only trusts his judgment, and anyone who believes that the work should be done differently is frowned upon. This leads to a lack of organizational growth and individuals because the work is done similarly even when innovations are possible. Employees are not allowed to develop their skills; instead, they are forced to follow the guidelines enforced by the micromanager.

As a manager, you should hire people only if you trust them. If you believe that workers slack off, you should build a work ethic that motivates them to work harder. Mostly when people are given independence, they tend to feel responsible for their work and finish it in time. All you should provide your team is constructive feedback from time to time, leaving them to decide the specifics of a project. Try not to see their mistakes as proof of why micromanaging works; instead, you should see it as opportunities for them to grow and become independent. Employees are just like you, they can be flawed at times, but that doesn't mean they shouldn't be trusted to do their job. They have been given their position because of a reason just like you. You should showcase to them that you believe in their judgment rather than questioning everything they do.

When you micromanage your employees, it makes them feel like they are not deserving of your trust, and that leads to demotivation. A lack of confidence can be detrimental for the whole organization because employees start second-guessing everything they do. They feel like they don't have the autonomy; they're not heard and are not connected to the organization. How the leaders of an organization behave is what makes employees leave – we have all heard of nightmare stories about bosses being too controlling. As an organization, you cannot afford to treat your employees like that because your business is entirely dependent on them.

Trusting your employees and giving them room to do their work makes the staff feel secure in their position. They feel like they are valued, that their inner needs are being recognized, and eventually, it makes them feel validated for their work, which is all any of us want. Freedom makes a hierarchal and sometimes oppressive structural organization method into one that makes people feel positive and secure rather than scared.

Micromanaging is the same as treating employees like little children who don't know what they are doing. Nobody likes being infantilized because it withdraws their rationality and makes them think that they are not being valued enough within the organization.

The best way to control your need to micromanage is to set up Key Performance Indicators (KPIs). KPIs are indicators that show if the workers are hitting the targeted numbers or not. You won't have to worry about the everyday work process for each one of your employees. Instead, at the end of the week, you can just check the data to see if the right amount of work has been done or not. For example, if your sales managers are achieving the goals set for them, there is no need to review their communication and sales strategies.

The biggest problem with micromanagement is that it will lead to your burnout. You can't assume that as a manager, you will always love your position and see it as a privilege rather than a curse. Once you start looking over every shoulder, it will make you feel paranoid because you have expanded your knowledge base. The more you become aware of the smallest component of what's happening in the work process on an average day, the more you will see places where things can go wrong. Eventually, you will start hating your job because you ended up doing everybody's work instead of just being a leader. Burnout from micromanagement will begin to impact your life outside of work as well. Calling your employees late at night to check on their work rather than just enjoying some free time with your family will end up making you feel anxious and depressed.

LEAD CORRECTLY

To transition from being a boss to a leader requires reevaluating your organizational values and approach. A boss believes in their capacity over the teams – this puts them in the center of the workplace, pushing those who do the work aside. Although a boss should believe in himself, when this belief becomes so absolute that nobody else is allowed to believe in their opinions and ideas, the workspace becomes toxic.

People want you to believe in them rather than you believing in yourself. They don't want their superiors to lord over them at all points; instead, they want encouragement that pushes them to perform better. You have to be aware of the position of power you occupy, which automatically legitimizes your words in the eyes of the employees. They look to you for a metric of their self-worth. So, when they submit a report to you, they are looking for you to make them feel more empowered and capable. But, when you start telling them what to do, they think that they can never get it right and will always be in the wrong. Employees who are unsure of themselves will reflect that in their work.

When managing people, you should enable workers to manage themselves. You should put in words of inspiration, give them opportunities to shine, and let them learn from their mistakes. This will allow them to feel capable and will help them fight against their self-doubt, allowing them to fulfill their tasks without their insecurities hindering them.

You should self-reflect where your bossiness comes from. Most bosses tend to enjoy the power trip, and that makes them continually prove to themselves that they do indeed deserve their position. Solidifying your position always comes at the cost of making someone else feel inferior – someone has to feel small for someone to feel big. This dialectical relationship guides the relationship between tyrannical bosses and employees. The only person this benefits is the boss's ego and not the organization – the organization suffers when the workers feel so unsure of themselves that the quality of their work starts to deplete. You have to confront your insecurities and see how they play out in the workplace.

Bad bosses tend to take credit for other people's work because they can't stand the fact that an employee came up with a good idea. This discourages employees from sharing their ideas with the team because they know they will only receive scorn from their superiors. A leader makes himself big and small when required and is not afraid to say that he might be wrong at times. This allows the team to grow as a whole unit because the leader's thoughts aren't central at all times, but instead, ideas work in rotation; whoever comes up with a great idea is rewarded for it, and everyone gets a chance to feel important.

You must ask yourself why you want to be a boss. Is it to personally fulfill your egotistical desires or to better the whole company? Leadership is all about tackling this misconception that managers tend to have by changing the values and ways of communicating within the organization. The end goal of a boss should be to foster a work culture that remains humane and does not become exploitative of the workers. While it is generally an agreed practice in business that profit should come before anything, leadership changes that and puts people before profits.

You should approach this question by simply asking why we are in business at all if it isn't supposed to serve other humans and the people who work within the company. Corralling a bunch of people together to achieve a commonly stated mission, in the end, has nothing to do with the boss and everything to do with the people involved. By following the principle of putting the company before the boss, what we do is change the metrics based on which business success is determined. Instead of profits and numbers, it becomes about overall employee and customer happiness. Contrary to popular beliefs, such a leadership method ends up making companies increase their profits because the employees feel like they are part of the team and not merely a tool in the bigger picture. This pushes them to dedicate themselves with their whole heart to their work they are doing.

To conclude, don't be bossy. Let go of your need for dominance and start empowering your employees; a smart leader sees that getting the work done exemplarily is what helps the organization. As a boss, your value is connected to the work of your employees, so you will be better off by treating them well and ensuring they have the right mental capacity to perform their best. Here's what you can do not to be bossy:

Be Understanding: The tired old rule of management is that there are no excuses when it comes to working. The important question here is, what counts as an excuse? In most cases, it's the inability of employees to complete their work. If we take a deeper look into this problem, what we discover is that there are always good reasons why employees aren't able to do the tasks assigned to them. If you think about it, employees are always scared they will lose their job or be reprimanded if they don't finish their work, and that should ideally result in a situation where all work is completed in time.

So, why does that not happen? Because your employees are not perfect little robots, they are human beings. What comes in the middle of work getting done are their problems and the feelings associated with that. To address this problem, you have to be understanding as a leader. You must see where the employee's problems are emanating from. Understanding is all about listening to the employee instead of dismissing their inability to function properly as an excuse. Once you see the reason behind their subpar performance, you will be able to address their issues or at least help them through it, ensuring the successful completion of the task.

Be Empathetic: Empathy is the ability to relate to somebody else and their feelings, almost as if you saw through their eyes – to feel their discomfort as if it was your own. It's like putting yourself in some-body's shoes and humanizing them by understanding what they are feeling and what makes them who they are. This helps you get why people behave a certain way instead of just dismissing their behavior as something you don't want to engage with.

The biggest problem with empathetic thinking is that most people shy away from it because it makes them feel uncomfortable. Completely understanding someone else's pain, especially as a leader whose job is to expect results without caring about how it's done, can lead to a sort of cognitive dissonance. On the one hand, you know why somebody is struggling to do their work, while on the other hand, your job is to ensure they do their work no matter what. This is where empathic leadership comes in – you have to find a balance between these two and act as a friend to take care of the other person's feelings, and ensuring that they complete their work.

The other tricky part of empathy is that many people confuse it with how they would feel in somebody's shoes. Instead of under-standing what somebody else is going through, many people simply dismiss those feelings as not real and just think that the other person should act differently. Learning empathy is about realizing that people can't help feeling the way they do, and by not addressing those feel-ings, you're asking them to put themselves through even more pain.

Ask How You Empower Them: The employees know what is holding them back, and by just asking them what they need, you have started on the first step of empowering your workers. Empowerment is allowing the worker's true potential to rise. You can do this by dele-gating work to them, hearing their inputs, guiding them throw the problems in the work process, giving them constructive feedback and eventually, training them to become self-reliant. Empowerment is not a single day process; it requires you to push your workers to speak up and register their voice. Getting your employees to trust you enough so they can be honest with you and then doing what they want is how you empower people.

Your task as a manager should be to show your workers how to get things done. Once this is completed, take a step back and trust them to see it through. An autonomous workforce is required to come up with solutions themselves rather than going to the manager with every small problem. This will result in self-reliant workers who don't need to be bossed around to get them to complete the goals they are supposed to achieve. Be a leader and guide, don't command!

CHAPTER 3

THE ESSENTIALS TO UNDERSTAND LEADERSHIP IN TODAY'S WORLD

L eadership isn't a bubble anymore; decisions now replicate across borders and don't just concern a section of the population, but the whole planet. Innovation has become the key to success because we have become so connected on a global scale that you have to adapt, or you risk getting forgotten. Standing out as a leader has become even more complicated, gone are the day of simply giving fancy speeches and hoping your employees do their best.

A leader in the current times faces many challenges and has to be well versed in conversation, politics, environmental activism, and social justice. The expectations put on a leader nowadays are a lot because you are a representative of your company. People don't see corporations as private entities beyond reproach anymore; they want their corporations to be ethical, to listen to the consumers, and be active within the community.

A leader has to be aware of the diversity of opinions and experiences that surround them. Managers have to learn how they can dismantle systematic biases that exist within the framework of the corporate setup. That means addressing essential issues like women's rights and discrimination to ensure that your company doesn't fall behind. You have to follow modern values if you want to be successful because that's what your customers and employees want from you.

With the advent of technology, everyone is empowered because of the wide variety of information that is available to everyone. Knowledge formulates what expectations employees have from their work, and today's generation is better versed with their social and political heritage than the older ones. The need of the hour is adaptability because if you aren't changing, some other company is. If you don't want to be left behind, you have to study the socio-political climate outside of the workplace itself and align your business accordingly.

With these changes in our material environment, there is also a change in the consciousness of workers. Attention spans have become smaller, and people want to consume things all the time. We live in a fast-paced world, and everyone craves movement; they want a job that offers development and excitement. The new-age worker looks like this:

Does Not Like Desk Jobs: It's not someone who wants to work long hours and do unexciting, boring desk jobs. They want to be challenged and do things that push them to think outside of their work. They are hard workers, but at the same time, they like to compress their jobs to shorter periods. This happens because they want to be done with their work as soon as possible so they can have some time off to do what they want to.

As a leader, you have to accept this method of work rather than pushing people to work more than their attention span can handle. People have short motivations these days, and their mind flutters around looking for the new thing that interests them. When your employees get to work in shorter periods, they will work fast and hard, getting everything done effectively. Pushing them to contribute their free time will only make them hate their job.

Jobs with More Possibilities: The new-age worker wants more access to the possibilities life can have. Unlike the earlier generations who are more than happy even to have a job, the new generation has an accentuated sense of self. This self-belief is an important aspect of their personality because they all think they are special and deserve whatever they want. This is an essential attitude to understand because it means they are not going to be put down and pigeonholed by their bosses. People are willing to take risks, now more than ever, and if you try to restrict their dreams, they will leave your organization to make their own way.

When employees are aware of the possibilities life can hold for them, they want to do anything to achieve them. You should communicate with your employees to realize what inspires them and where they wish to go. By understanding their story, you can direct them in the workplace in a way that aligns their motivation for self-growth with the company's goals. All you need to do is channel their aspirations along the right track by guiding them, and they will succeed.

Informed and Knowledgeable: Employees these days are highly aware of the social landscape. They know what they want from life; they understand what self-respect means and how they should be treated. Bosses, for the longest time, have been this group of people who saw themselves as above the herd of dimwit employees, but that's changed now. The manager might be an expert in organizing people, but it is the worker who has all the information and knowledge that the company needs to thrive. This knowledge is their power because, in the modern world, it is technocratic and technical knowledge about the specifics of work that leads to success. Such well-educated workers who have done multiple degrees, know how to do their job and channel their creativity.

As a leader, you have to treat these people with respect and recognize their knowledge as a valuable resource for the organization. By giving them autonomy over their workspace and allowing them to lead projects, you will push them to share their expertise with the whole team so that everyone can benefit from it. For getting them to do this, you must create a level of trust that goes beyond simplistic employer-employee relationships. Take your time to get to know your employees deeply and frankly.

Understand their strengths and weaknesses, find out what drives them to do their job, and ask them about their fears and the challenges they face. Understanding each employee has to happen beyond the scope of formal aptitude and personality tests. This will allow you to use the knowledge of your employees while orchestrating discussions and meetings. You can even delegate important roles to them so that you don't have to micromanage the team. It will also ease your burden because you will be assured that someone with knowledge and expertise is in a directional role.

Millennials: There is a gradual shift in workforce demographics with younger generations entering the workforce at a rapid pace, while other ones slowly move toward retirement. This change presents a unique opportunity as well as challenges for managers. The newer generation has different attitudes toward work, leadership, technology, etc. To become a successful business, you have to be aware of the nuances of what expectations the newer generation has from their managers.

The biggest difference between earlier generations, such as baby boomers and millennials, is their attitude toward work. Earlier generations grew up on a heavy dose of believing the world was a hard place, and weakness had no place in our society. They were told they have to sacrifice for the greater good, and if they want to be successful in this world, they must accept that only the fit survive, and those who complain get left behind.

The current generation is the complete opposite – they don't believe they should sacrifice their desires for anybody else, especially for companies they believe exist to serve them. You can see this clash in the "participation trophy" debate – many older people think that the current generation has been praised for doing the bare minimum and hence, have a softer outlook toward life. But, the fact of the matter is that the newer generation believes they all deserve to be appreciated, and nobody should be left behind.

The difference in these attitudes can be noticed in simple things like baby boomers believing that unpaid overtime hours are an essential part of work and should not be protested against. While millennials not just hate being forced to work more than required, they want to be paid more for the time they do work.

THIS IS HOW MILLENNIALS DIFFER FROM PAST GENERATIONS

Diversity: As a generation, they value diversity the most. Not just in terms of variety of opinions, but also sexuality, gender identity, race, etc. Unlike the previous generations, millennials are all about self-expression – they don't want to conform to the standards set by society, but like to challenge them instead. They march to the beat of their drum.

They also have a general attitude that accepts and celebrates differences. They are extremely intolerant toward discrimination of any form and are politically active enough to register their opinions. They crave understanding and are open to exploring the different experiences that shape the psyche of each individual. As a manager, you have to take care that you empathize with them and try to get where they are coming from.

Tech-Driven: They are also tech-driven. Younger people are more comfortable working on their laptops and require a technically up-to-date workspace. They also rely far more on communication through technology, so you should ensure that your workplace has upgraded itself and can function completely online. A change in technology also leads to a change in how the workspace is calibrated. While earlier, the workplace had a physical boundary, now it extends beyond just physical space and exists virtually for anyone to access. Many people now prefer to work remotely and don't like adhering to fixed working hours. As a manager, it is your job to ensure that your workspace is flexible enough to adapt to these changes.

· · ·

Individualists: Millennials are individualists, and what they crave is autonomy because they don't like being told what to do. They want to maintain their personal space, and this extends to the workplace. As a manager, you have to be careful not to seem controlling because that will make them distrust you. You should be open and transparent with them about everything, all decisions should include every employee, and there should be no kind of favoritism.

Analytical and Discerning: Millennials are more discerning and analytical. It means that they aren't stupid enough just to accept your word simply because you are the boss. Unlike previous generations, they don't respond well to authority but are actively critical of it. They are easily able to spot when they are being manipulated and exploited. Millennials won't accept your authority just because it's socially legitimized by an institution. If they are bold enough to question the fundamental conceptions of previously accepted things, then they are smart enough to question a socially constructed title that constitutes the position of being a 'boss.'

Don't Care Too Much About Money: They don't care as much about money as previous generations and hence, aren't likely to just do any job as long as it pays well. What the new generation wants is a job they care about because they are driven by passion rather than superficiality. Money is enough to make people do the bare minimum, but that's not how organizations thrive. If you want a company where people give their all, come up with innovative solutions and participate in ensuring the success of the organization.

You need to fulfill the newer generation's desire to be more engaged with their work. This can only happen if they feel like their hard work is being appreciated, their need for validation and appreciation is being met, and their leader supports them.

. . .

Crave Empathy: Millennials crave empathy because they have grown up with all their needs being met. They have been allowed to dream, and their worldview is one of a sensitive world where everyone takes care of each other.

Older leadership techniques of using fear as a motivator will not work on them. Fear is a great pusher, but not a creative stimulator – it's empathy that stimulates people to care more about their work. If your staff sees you as a friend who will hear them rather than a dictator who will fire them if they don't give the expected results, then they will feel more inclined to provide you with their best efforts.

Caring is a two-way street – if your employees start to believe you care about them, they will care about you too. And they will learn to demonstrate this care through their work.

Once you realize the characteristics that comprise the newer generation, which you have to lead, you have to do a bit of self-reflection and change your values.

WHAT IT TAKES FOR YOU AS A LEADER:

Adapt: Adapting means putting your own opinions in the backdrop and relearning how to lead. If you want to understand millennials, start with yourself. Think about the values you have and why they might be problematic. Once you know where your values are coming from and how you have perhaps been socialized into thinking only in a certain way, you'll be able to open up your mind to new possibilities of what the world can look like. This should have an added impact on your leadership style, method of communication, and treatment of employees. You have to accept diversity as a given rather than trying to control what the workspace looks like. At the end of the day, the employees are as important as you and as entitled to their worldview as you. You have to learn to coexist with them to ensure there is no friction.

The bottom line is that you have no option but to do this. If you remain outdated in your values, then you will become an obsolete leader. Millennials are already in the workforce and are at the forefront of changing what work looks and feels like. After that, another generation that is even more independent and self-assured is going to come, called Generation Z. They are the kids who grew up on the Internet, and they have been exposed to a multitude of opinions and experiences. They are diverse and open in their thinking, so you should be too.

Cognitive evolution has led to a complexity of viewpoints coming to the center of all discourse. People think about everything they encounter now; they don't just ignore a boss being rude to them but dismantle the entire structure that legitimizes and permits such behavior to take place. If you still believe in outdated ideas of doing business, your opinions will lose all value in front of your employees. You have to keep up or get left behind.

Ultimately the lesson here is that it's not about you at all, it's about the people who are following you, they are more important:

All employees have certain expectations from their bosses, and when they aren't met, people become dissatisfied. You are the living embodiment of what the company stands for and values, so you have to understand what your following expects from a leader. Being a leader is about being a chameleon; you have to be approachable for every person and should meet their expectations. This requires you to be non-judgmental until the point where you are constantly the one taking a backseat. Let your employees do the talking and just guide them according to the way they want to be guided.

You should ask yourself if your following feels empowered or not – do they think their leader helps them do better and is like a rock they can depend on? Or is their leader another problem they have to tackle in the workspace to get to their true potential?

Could they do it without you? The question itself should not alarm you because a good leader should learn to erase themselves from the scene. If you have done your job well as a leader, your following should be able to work without needing you at all. Of course, this is not likely to occur because everyone needs direction and a point of communication. Still, if you have taught your team well, they should be able to acquire the necessary skills required to work autonomously.

Your following is your biggest asset. A leader derives his energy and his power from the people who believe in his command. You are only a leader if there is a team; without one, you won't be able to achieve anything. You want your team to be in your corner supporting you rather than working against you.

In today's world, people expect a lot from their leaders. Your job is to be receptive enough to catch on to these expectations and embody them. Here are the things you should keep in mind if you want to be a leader people want to work for:

Consistent Communication: Consistent communication means being clear and concise about the messages you give to your employees. Lack of openness makes people feel confused and unsure, which hurts their productivity. People in positions of power try to lessen the amount they communicate. Do not make the mistake of shortening interactive meetings and cutting down one-to-one time.

The way you use your words can determine how you are viewed. If your words are impactful, people will relate to them on an emotional level. The better you are at communication, the more you can prove your authenticity. As a communicator, you must strive to be lucid. People should be able to grasp the meaning of your words. If you are not clear about what you want from them, they can mess up and feel disconnected from you. Your ability to empathize and understand what people want makes you a good leader.

Recognition and Praise: According to *Entrepreneur*, only 35 percent of employees said a raise is what they need, while 65 percent said what they are looking for is praise. Many employees feel disconnected from their employers, and that impacts their work ethic. When people work, they create something, and they want recognition for that. Whenever we do some work, we want to display it, and we want everyone to know about it and appreciate us for it. When you don't pay attention to the work done by your employees, they feel that they aren't being appreciated enough and lose motivation.

Everyone wants to be recognized in different ways, some people like to be celebrated, and other people just want an email. It's crucial to change your recognition system based on the individual needs of the employees.

Skill Development: People love a leader who is invested not just in getting them to do the work but personally in their overall growth. All employees want to learn the tricks of the trade, which is why they are looking to build personal connections with their managers so they can mentor them.

You should always be on the lookout for opportunities where you can teach your employees a new skill, get them to attend a training session, or just generally give them some constructive feedback. This will encourage your employees to stay within the organization and help it grow by developing themselves.

Designed Work Culture: Workplace culture isn't random but systematically created by managers to make their employees feel like they are part of a community. The most important part of this is to find a team that works well together. What you should look for in employees is how much they align with the values and work ethics of your organization. You should try your hardest to retain the right team members and phasing out those who aren't right for the organization. When there is a team member who is not up to the mark, it frustrates the other team members because they have to pull their weight as well. A weak team member can destroy everyone's motivation to work, so make sure that you hire the right people.

After you have done this, also ensure that people get the job roles they are most likely to excel in. When people are forced to do work they don't like, they feel alienated and uninspired. Their creativity can feel restraint; your job as a leader is to channel their skills and talents in the right direction.

Acceptance of Failure: When failure is seen as something to be avoided at all costs, employees will work because of fear, not because they want to. It also hinders people's ability to think creatively and innovate because they start to believe that taking risks is going to result in them being punished. Nobody in your team should feel like they're going to be left behind just because they failed at something once. Create a safe space for people to let their insecurities and failures out. This will allow everyone not to see work as a competitive space, but one that is filled with support. Encouragement is always better than a daunting fear to motivate people.

Clear Vision: If you're a leader who doesn't have a goal that he can sell to his employees, it's like the blind leading the blind. First, you must learn how to create a positive vision that motivates you to get up in the morning. And then you have to share that vision with your employees – this doesn't just mean talking to them or emailing them about it. You must ensure that the vision that's in your head translates to your employees and is as meaningful for them as it is for you, and motivates them to achieve that goal.

Emphasizing Accountability: All leaders like to hold their staff accountable, but many don't apply the same standard to themselves. This means recognizing that the team's failure is a reflection of your bad management skills as well. Just like it is okay for employees to fail and learn from it, it's okay for you to use the same approach. If you refuse to believe that you could have been in the wrong, you will never learn and update your management strategy, repeating the same mistakes of the past.

Contrary to what most bosses believe, accepting that you can be mistaken doesn't make your team respect your authority any less. It makes them trust you more because they know that you are flawed like them. This will allow your employees to feel comfortable in the workspace and not be worried about what you might think about them.

Many leaders think that if they're going to be held accountable, they should take more time to think. This can lead to an analysis-paralysis because you will end up overthinking everything you do. Not being afraid to make mistakes also means doing everything without assuming what will happen afterward. As a leader, you have to be quick on your feet and showcase fast decision-making skills to help guide your team. You should be confident about the decisions you make, and if they go wrong, then so be it, learn and do better.

Honesty: Many leaders think they know better than their employees, and that's why it's okay for them not to be completely honest with them about the functions of the business. Trust works both ways; if you expect your team to follow you blindly, you should also be honest with them even when the truth might be inconvenient for you. When people perceive they are being lied to, they don't recover from it easily and will leave the organization no matter what you say to them. Instead, when you are honest with them, they will appreciate that even more, and it will increase their trust in your direction.

People Come First: Productivity doesn't come from pushing people; it only happens when your employees are happy. A good leader recognizes that the internal state of the employees impacts their work. A frustrated and angry employee, who has been made to work all week, isn't being paid enough and doesn't feel respected will not want to work at all. Most businesses think that profits are the most important thing, but successful companies understand that it's people who matter the most. An organization is essentially just people, and they are the ones who generate value. If they aren't satisfied, there won't be any profits.

· · ·

Manage in Every Direction: Generally, leaders only like to think of organizing and directing those who are directly below them. A good leader understands that managing has to function in all directions – it's your duty to handle the communication of your subordinates with your fellow managers and seniors, for them. You have to manage down, up, and sideways if you want effective communication within the organization and the timely redressal of problems. Your employees will thank you for this because they might not be as familiar with the other seniors in the organization and hence, would not be able to communicate well with them. Your support will mean the world to them because it will allow your employees to feel confident even in front of senior management.

Team Building: A focus on team building is of paramount importance. Team building is about creating a work culture where everyone feels like they are part of a larger community. Instead of each worker seeing themselves as only individuals, members of a team see each other as interchangeable in their roles. They feel accountable for each other's success, and this makes them feel responsible for everyone completing their tasks rather than just finishing what they have to do and going home.

An essential component of this is people liking each other because, when people enjoy each other's company, it makes work easier for them. They feel supported by their peers – an individual employee can sometimes feel stuck in their work, unable to find the motivation to finish what they have to do. But when they have a whole team behind, their friends, they find subsistence and energy in the team spirit.

Team spirit is the sense of unity that employees feel – it allows them to feel connected to their job, company, peers, and work. When people feel like they're part of something greater than them, it allows the employees to feel fulfilled. When people feel fulfilled, they're likely to work better. It also makes them selfless, as they start to help others out with their task or take on extra work just to see the company rise.

If you want dedicated employees, you have to start team-building. However, you can't just make people feel like they're part of a team by taking all your employees out to lunch every few days. You have to make them think they're all alike and think similarly. To create this sense of unity, get some matching t-shirts, cups, and other things that remind them that they're part of the team. Things represent our feelings, and we form meaning through them; by giving people something that reminds them of the group they're a part of, you'll keep their team spirit alive.

Eventually, team building will lead to effective communication within the organization leading to an increase in productivity. Any misunderstanding or problems will be easily solved when everyone likes each other and is willing to sort out their differences.

Work-Life Balance: Unlike earlier times, when employees were expected to prioritize their work over their life, the newer generation prefers the opposite. They don't live life to work but work so they can do what they want. Employees nowadays are not afraid to admit this and will make it very clear to you that they aren't available outside of work to fulfill your demands. You can't just call people up at any time now and expect them to tackle problems. Once work is done, people want to be left alone and don't want a boss who disturbs their time alone.

You should get ahead of this and fulfill this desire of your employees by giving them enough time to do what they want. If they want to go on a vacation and spend time with their family, you should encourage it. In the long run, this will allow your employees to take a breather and come back to work with a refreshed zeal and dedication.

A neat trick you can use is making work seem less like work and more like enjoyment. Many startups have workplace environments that are relaxed, have no boundaries or walls, have beanbags to lounge on, and break rooms to play games in. This makes the experience of work feel less taxing. Contrary to popular belief, this doesn't make employees less productive but makes them believe they're not working at all. When it starts to feel like a nice chilling spot, people don't feel mentally fatigued and remain motivated throughout the day. It also pushes employees to work for longer hours because they want to stay there.

The work environment also impacts your mood – nobody wants to feel like his or her work is a dingy prison where he or she has to stare at bare gray walls all day. They want to feel like they're part of something cool, and by giving them the right space, you can stimulate their mood toward enjoying work.

Equal Workspace: Everyone's nightmare office is one where the manager has a separate and better working space, where you are not allowed to go in unless it's with express permission. Segregating the workspace like that embeds hierarchy into the minds of your employees. Instead of seeming like an approachable person, you start to look like someone who people should be wary of.

Instead, you have to develop a workspace of equality where it seems like you are one of the masses. You shouldn't show that you have special privileges and are above everyone else. If you want your employees to treat you like a friend whom they can share anything with you, have to act like it too.

The biggest hurdle toward effective and clear communication is hierarchization. When people feel like somebody has more power than them, they instantly distrust them. No matter what you do after that to make yourself seem approachable, your employees will always hesitate to share their true opinions and inputs. You want your employees to speak whatever is in their mind without thinking of any possible negative consequences. This can only happen if they feel comfortable enough to let their guards down. It's your job to ensure that everyone sees the workplace as a safe space where they can let their positive and negative aspects hangout.

Sharing is what determines the success of a workplace, and people only want to share when they feel like their superiors validate their emotions. You can't have loyalty within your organization if you don't respect people's feelings – without personalized relationships, people have no incentive to care about the company and its leaders.

The problem with business leaders is that many of them believe emotions are weak, and being empathetic will lead to their employees losing respect for them. They think that leadership is about making believe in their authority, and any sign of emotions will make people perceive them as weak, leading to disarray and anarchy. Today's world is a more emotionally expressive one, and you have to adapt yourself to it if you want to be a good leader.

CHAPTER 4

HOW EMOTIONAL INTELLIGENCE IS A GAME CHANGER

With more and more employees from the younger generation entering the management workforce, there has been a significant change in the work culture. Today, more than ever, it exists an emphasis on creating a space for people's emotions in the workspace. There are two major reasons for this change. Firstly, the new generation of workers is more sensitive. They care deeply about the environment that they are in and have idealistic values. Secondly, not only are they sensitive, but they are also aware of their own emotions and their emotional need. This, in turn, gives them a heightened sense of situational awareness and the emotions of others. The more they feel like they exist in an emotionally fulfilling environment, the likelier they are to dedicate themselves to the task at hand completely.

The transformation in the workforce means that the role of the boss is also changing. Traditionally, the traits associated with a good boss would be a savvy business sense, sound analytical skills, diverse experience, and ambition. However, as a boss of the new generation, you will only be viewed as capable of being a good manager if you can also sensitively look after the emotional environment of your workplace and the emotional wellbeing of your subordinates.

The one trait, which unites most successful bosses today, is a high emotional intelligence (also referred to as EQ). Unless you can evolve with the times and master this trait, you will get left behind in the leadership race. It is statistically proven that young workers are much more likely to quit a job that doesn't cater to their emotional needs since they have more options and mobility in the job market than the past generations.

According to the *2018 Employee Engagement and Retention statistics* by Access Perks, 12% of employees would quit their job if they did not feel appreciated, and 30% would consider changing their job if they felt unhappy at work. More importantly, nearly 60% of workers claimed that they would move to an alternative offering lower pay if they got the chance to work with a great boss. It is essential to become aware of what EQ is and how to master it if you want to become the kind of boss that workers look forward to working with.

WHAT IS EMOTIONAL INTELLIGENCE?

Emotional intelligence or Emotional Quotient (EQ) refers to the ability of an individual to identify and manage one's own emotions and, subsequently, the emotions of others. An emotionally intelligent individual can comprehend and control his feelings while remaining open to the feelings of others and positively responding to them. This awareness is not only limited to positive emotions but also negative ones - emotions like frustration, sadness, envy, anger, or other. Individuals who are in touch with their emotions are also tuned to the feelings that other people may experience in different situations.

EQ vs. IQ: To put it simply, Emotional Intelligence (or Emotional Quotient-EQ) is as important as Intelligence Quotient (IQ) in a successful person and leader, but these two are very different traits. IQ is related to the logical reasoning and intellectual ability of the individual. It determines your ability to learn, understand, and implement knowledge, intuitive thinking, or 'common sense.'

People with a high IQ can overcome challenging analytical tasks, conduct adequate research, and come up with quick solutions. EQ, on the other hand, is related to the capability of the individual to identify and assess emotions and use those emotions as a central part of their analytical thinking. It is essential for generating team spirit, encouraging collaboration, and maintaining successful relations with other people. People with high EQ are adept at overcoming social challenges and creating good emotional environments for themselves. This quality is found in successful leaders, captains, and managers.

Emotional Intelligence can be divided into four parts.

Self-Awareness: A key concept that often comes up in discussions about Emotional Intelligence is self-awareness. It is the ability to identify and comprehend your moods and motivations, and the effect they have on the people around you. Having an awareness of the situations and stimuli that can trigger feelings of rage and loss of control in you will help you navigate those triggers better so that you do not come across as a leader who is prone to outbursts.

Any loss of control often comes from a place of lacking empathy. Being self-aware ensures that you can face adverse situations while remaining respectful of other people's boundaries and stay polite and collected. Self-awareness is a sign of self-reflection, which means that a leader is listening to feedback and constantly introspecting to improve everyone's performance.

Maturity: Closely linked to the idea of a cool temperament is maturity. Maturity is not simply about being reserved and objective as a leader, it is indicative of a much deeper emotional trait that's related to a lack of selfishness and ego. Leaders with lower emotional quotients tend to erase the efforts of their subordinates in the workplace and put themselves at the center of things. This comes across as an immature trait, which encourages feelings of distrust and lack of respect in your workers. A mature leader is aware of how to use his knowledge to help others while not making a show of his power, and how to make people feel included and involved. Such a leader can handle business and personal situations with dignity. This transforms the oppressive image of the boss into the image of a leader who can be relied upon for everything, from advice to morale-boosting.

Social Skills: Not only challenging but also awkward situations can often come up in a place of work. This can range from subtle friction to blown-out conflicts that result from clashing personalities of workers. Resolving such situations doesn't always need a dominating or extremely formal approach. To strengthen communication and encourage healthy patterns of praise and criticism among subordinates, a leader needs a high level of empathy and deep personal knowledge about the emotional capacity of all his employees. Navigating these situations means implementing a lot of the things that you have learned as an emotionally aware leader. Your insight into a conflict is key to diffusing it in a way that satisfies all parties involved, as well as sets a good precedent for your workers to follow.

Rapport: The amount of emotional intelligence you have will likely reflect on the kind of energy you and your workplace projects. If you tend to the emotional needs of your workers, you will create channels for smooth communication between them. If you successfully make people feel heard, you can help them build relationships that are not based on cold competition but on the rapport they share by working for the same common goal. This kind of a mutually supportive relationship means that many smaller frictions will get smoothed out on their own. A good rapport can create a fun working environment so that workers look forward to interacting with their leader and their co-workers.

BENEFITS OF EMOTIONAL INTELLIGENCE

A high EQ is beneficial not only to the potential leader but to every average person. Individuals with high EQ have better communication skills, less anxiety in social situations, less likelihood to aggravate conflicts, greater empathy in relationships, and lower levels of general stress. This means that they find it easier to overcome lives many challenges and maintain a successful personal life while aspiring for success in their career. Emotional intelligence directly influences our behavior – how we treat ourselves when we are alone and how we treat others around us. Hence it is key to crafting a warm, trustworthy, fun, and strong personality.

Emotional Intelligence in Leaders: As a leader, however, a high EQ can make you shine and set you apart from other managers. It helps you look beyond the nitty-gritty parts of the management machine and at the larger emotional consequences that a boss can have on a workplace. As society becomes more and more complex and corporate tasks expand, along with the workforce, leaders must be able to effectively translate requirements and issues to their staff, paying close attention to all avenues of communication. While adopting emotional intelligence as an approach to leadership is a big shift from earlier managerial strategies that are mostly about running a tight ship, there is an increasing recognition that happiness is central to productivity for the modern worker.

Leaders are learning that they need to put the needs of their employees first, and that is how they will accrue the most benefits for their endeavors in the long run. Emotional intelligence, therefore, impacts both the leader and the whole organization.

WHY ARE EMOTIONALLY INTELLIGENT LEADERS SUCCESSFUL?

Leaders with higher emotional intelligence are better leaders because they display a sounder decision-making sense. Since they are more internally aware of their weaknesses, they tend to make more efforts not to cover up their shortcomings and mistakes. Instead, they trust other people with the tasks that they are weak at. This encourages trust among co-workers and humanizes the boss in the eyes of his subordinates, which makes honest conversations possible.

Such leaders are also less likely to fall prey to any impulsive decision making because they are critical of their aggravated emotional states. They self-regulate their anger and their frustrations better so that they don't unfairly lash out on their employees. Such leaders prioritize empathy over everything else and make an effort to get to know their employees. This attitude motivates employees to view their work as more than just a heavy burden and instead as something that they are being trusted to do because of their individual set of skills.

Employees of such leaders also grow more because they are given a sensitive, comfortable environment where feedback and criticisms flow healthily. Emotionally intelligent leaders are also quick to assess the tone of the situation and then match it to resolve any tensions that might prop up to keep up the spirit of collaborative work. Lastly, such leaders always have a better work-life balance because they pre-emptively deal with stressful situations and don't let their emotions overpower either their home or their work life. They are not consumed by their stress and therefore treat the people around them better.

HOW EMOTIONALLY INTELLIGENT LEADERS IMPACT ORGANIZATIONS

Companies and organizations which have been around for a long time often have well-established channels of information through which they receive their technical skills and knowledge. Such companies can still struggle with employee satisfaction, retention, and overall growth because they don't pay enough attention to their emotional intelligence. Companies with higher emotional intelligence empower better engagement between team members.

If they are anchored by an emotionally intelligent leader, employees form more positive associations with the process of teamwork. Team members who feel like they have a valued role in the collaborative process are more productive than those who do not have any personal attachment to their position. There is also an overall difference in the company culture when open communication is encouraged among people. They form stronger relationships, and while this was tradition-ally viewed as a weakness, for the companies of today, it can become the ultimate strength.

When the organization functions as a close-knit unit, they are more performance-driven. This ultimately benefits the company because each employee is not dedicating his energy only to fulfilling his personal career goals, but is actually investing in the success of his whole team, his trustworthy leader and ultimately the organization at large. In *Humble Leadership: The Power of Relationships, Openness, and Trust*, Edgar H. Schein and Peter A. Schein write, "In our view, leadership is always a relationship, and truly successful leadership thrives in a group culture of high openness and high trust."

TRAINING YOUR EQ

It is important to understand that not everyone is naturally inclined to being emotionally aware. The circumstances that we are put in as children and the kind of emotional environment we have at home can all impact our emotional intelligence as adults. Studies show that people who grew up in homes that were more emotionally open have higher EQ levels as adults. They are more sensitive to their peers and less afraid of asserting their emotional state and their emotional needs.

Similarly, individuals who have grown up in an environment where displaying emotions were discouraged; they are less likely to make emotions important to their leadership strategy. They also do not feel comfortable imagining others around them in an emotional light.

Emotional awareness can only be learned with patience. Most people like to dismiss others and their feelings in work situations. After all, they believe emotions belong outside the workspace. This separation between the employee and the person is a complete lie because, as human beings, we can't separate our different identities according to the space we inhabit.

If you're going through bad mental or physical health, the need to keep those personal problems outside of work is itself an oppressive demand to make that further enlarges the problem. Emotional sensitivity can only be cultivated when we start to become kind toward others and patient toward their needs. As a leader, you occupy a position of power, which means that your emotions are the dominant ones in the room – if you decide in a meeting to be cold and rational, everyone will have to follow that. So, set an example by being kind toward others and opening the space for personal discussions so the meeting can be more fruitful.

If you think that your EQ isn't good enough, the first step is to acknowledge this instead of dismissing it. Train yourself to think about others, to be patient, not to deny other people's feelings, and to hear what other people are thinking without questioning their motives or intents. You have to develop a caring attitude within yourself – go out of your way to ask others about what problems they are facing and how their life is going.

Your emotional awareness is also dependent on your mental and physical health; if you're tired and angry, it becomes harder to empathize with others, and that's fine. As long as you take the time to process your own emotions, you won't delegitimize other people. You don't need to feel guilty if you snap sometimes and aren't considerate, it happens to the best of us – being emotionally aware is not the same as being nice and reassuring all the time. You can have tough conversations with people while still acknowledging their feelings.

However, whether it is out of personal desire or the ambition to be a better leader, you can always train your EQ and make it better. Anyone can outgrow their bringing-up by actively working to define their personality. This kind of will power to be a better person is also a highly valuable quality in any boss. While IQ is harder to change since it is dependent on intellectual aptitude, EQ can be raised with enough practice and training.

The key thing to remember when training is that it is a very self-conscious process in which you have to slowly encourage your mind to be more aware and alert to the emotional tone of every situation. Firstly, you have to begin by paying more attention to your feelings and how it is affecting your behavior. Try to do this often, assessing your feelings to a variety of situations you are exposed to daily. Then, focus on the subtle or obvious ways in which the people around you shift their behavior in response to your emotions. For example, if you notice that people look visibly nervous when you feel angry, then there is a clear connection between your anger and their discomfort, which most likely projects you as an intimidating or aggressive person. By doing this simple exercise as much as you can, you will attain a sense of foresight by which you can predict your emotions and hence mitigate the possibility of losing control. This is the underlying principle of EQ training.

The EQ concept was introduced in the 1990s and has since seen much scientific research and work published around it. Some organizations have used data from these articles to create in-office culture, and coaching programs targeted at emotional intelligence, these are usually called interpersonal training or soft-skill training. From years of scientific work and practice, five main points can be made about emotional intelligence training:

EQ levels are solid, but not inflexible.

As said above, our EQ levels are determined by many different factors. Hence, people tend to believe that they mostly remain stable over the years. However, it is possible to improve our EQ levels over the long term with a lot of dedication in the right direction. It is mostly dependent on your willingness to put any effort into it.

Take a moment and try to imagine some of the worst bosses and managers that you've worked with. You will see that there is a set of negative behaviors that you can avoid from the get-go, but what is more difficult is to change your level of emotional intelligence internally. This is where maturity becomes important. Many times, in a position of leadership, you will have to internally resolve or face your negative emotions so that they don't negatively affect your subordinates. It is found that EQ tends to increase as people become older and more mature.

Coaching Programs Can be Effective

Don't be fooled; there are no programs that are a hundred percent effective in completely raising someone's EQ; an adequately designed and well-crafted coaching program can achieve significant improvement in interpersonal skills and stress management, up to 25% and 35% respectively. A coaching program can teach emotional intelligence as negotiation skills and social etiquette, using the malleability of the social mind and making it more kind, compassionate, and comfortable with social situations. These workplace EQ coaching programs look after your overall mental health and help you create higher levels of happiness.

The Importance of Feedback

There are many aspects of a good coaching program. Not only does it need extremely skilled and patient coaches, but it also needs to be customized to the kind of job environment the concerned individual is working in. The most important part of any coaching program is feedback. Many people who undergo such programs are unaware of how their moods and actions are perceived by others, even when they are highly motivated and intelligent. Your perception of yourself is likely to be clouded with your ambition and over-confidence, or your sense of competitiveness. Receiving honest feedback from a qualified coach through reliable personality tests can produce effective outcomes in EQ coaching.

The same goes for feedback of a book. Once you finished reading, I would really appreciate if you leave an honest review.

Techniques and Coaches Have Different Levels of Effectiveness

According to some of the research available on coaching methods, the most effective techniques are found to be ones that use cognitive behavioral therapy. Such techniques focus on enhancing the psychological flexibility of the individual. This determines their ability to confront unwanted situations and retain a neutral, calm state of mind through meditation and relaxation exercises. However, EQ coaching cannot be reduced completely to technicalities, it also depends a lot on how talented the coach is.

Results Vary for Every Person

Even if the most tested methods are used by the most objectively talented coaches, some people will not show any observable changes in their emotional intelligence. This is mostly a fault of the individual being unresponsive to any suggestions for psychological improvement or being unenthusiastic about the idea itself. As mentioned repeatedly, improving your emotional intelligence is, first and foremost, a personal decision that you need to make and consciously work toward internally. Often, this requires deep introspection and confrontations with some difficult parts of yourself, which not everyone is willing to do. If you mentally decide to become a great, emotionally aware leader, it is the first step toward making these techniques effective.

Becoming the Best Boss

The purpose of working on your emotional intelligence is to always stay one step ahead of your team at all times, in emotional terms. This requires very high levels of observation and sensitivity. Your employees are not just people on your payroll; they are the group of people you are entrusting with one of the most important aspects of your life. Similarly, these are not people who just come to their jobs to earn their wages; they are always looking for the opportunity to grow, bond, and better themselves as people. If you adopt this fundamental attitude, you will realize why it is so important to treat them as humans more than workers and to treat your employees as a team that you have to both lead and coordinate. Since you are their boss, you hold a lot of power over their activities in the office. You should be careful to use that power for the overall betterment of the organization. Instead of using the traditional pyramid structure where orders flow from the top to the bottom, turn it into an equal space where everyone can put their best skills to play.

Accommodating Others' Emotions:Being emotionally aware of your employees does not necessarily mean that you need to know every aspect of their personal life and their individual motivations. As a leader, your job is to find out how your employees respond to the work environment and form a mental map of the best way to remove hurdles, and encourage collaboration in the office.

To do this, you should always be on the lookout for how members of your team respond to situations they are put in, and each person will react differently. For example, while some people love to work under heavy pressure and are always motivated by the stress of work and deadlines, other people will get more anxious by too much pressure and end up underperforming. Some employees will display a lot of patience while dealing with adversities, while others will let their panic get the better of them. Some workers will have more informal relationships with each other, while having more professional relationships with other people. All of this information will become important while you are delegating work, assigning people to groups, or simply trying to make your employees feel comfortable in their role.

You cannot expect to transform all your employees into just one kind of worker. This is neither possible nor desirable since it is the individual differences of a group of people that is their biggest strength as a unit. You need to project calmness and adjust to the tones of your employees in a way that is not too disruptive to their natural working style, while also being a gentle nudge in the right direction. Your emotional intelligence is vital in deciding the right balance between being assertive and relaxed from situation to situation.

Keeping Your Team Satisfied

Observing and maneuvering your employees into comfortable positions is not your only job as a leader. You need to ensure that the general atmosphere of the office is jovial while also not being lackadaisical. This is best achieved by keeping your team satisfied and happy with their work and progress. Apart from being open and approachable as a leader, there are many other ways you can use your emotional intelligence to satisfy your employees. The purpose of going the extra mile to keep your employees happy is to encourage them to reciprocate your commitment to the office. The more satisfied your employees are, the likelier they are to work harder at whatever job they are assigned. You will eliminate a lot of negative associations that can turn into hurdles for work progress. Dissatisfied employees are usually more distracted and less available for challenging work. If you can prevent them from feeling like their job is a burden, you will push them in the direction of treating it as an opportunity to grow.

How to Maintain Happiness at Work

According to the author of the bestselling book, "The Happiness Project," happy people are not only more productive, but they are also much more creative and innovative. They are resilient and easily come back from difficult positions. They have less anxiety around their everyday roles and hence can focus on new possibilities. Moreover, happy people experience less work-related burnout. They look forward to their interactions with you, their boss, and all their co-workers instead of finding ways to avoid crucial meetings and team-building activities. In a nutshell, happy employees are more present in their jobs, both mentally and physically. By applying what you learn about the emotional tone of your office, you can ensure that each employee can access this happy state of mind.

The most important aspect of satisfying your team is to recognize whenever your team-members make progress. It is not always adequate to have a points-based rewards system. You have to qualita-tively highlight when people overcome personal challenges or achieve new individual milestones. You must make employees feel like they belong in a shared space. For this, you have to authentically take an interest in the personal journey of your employees while they are under your wing. If your employees feel like they are getting all the tools that they need to succeed from their boss, they will be much more engaged at work.

Make interactions as less stressful as possible for everyone. People should focus more on effective communication than maintaining formal channels of communication that are devoted to hierarchies. Your employees should feel comfortable joking around with each other and with you. You should also encourage healthy practices like taking relaxing breaks, getting enough sleep, and healthy meals. While these things may seem too minimal to be noticeable, they go a long way in ensuring the general happiness of your company. Remember, that to be a good leader, you need to stop calculating everything and keeping a count of how much you do for each employee. Being emotionally aware is a part of your leadership style, not a business strategy.

Preventing Conflicts

A huge advantage of being an emotionally aware leader is that you will be able to predict more conflicts than ever. Your understanding of your employees will give you an intuitive sense of where friction could emerge. You will attain knowledge of how to deal with each employee based on what they respond to most effectively. You can assign work in a way that individuals with the most consistent working styles grouped, and those who are most likely to clash are placed in clearly defined, separate roles. Also, you could schedule fun team-building activities right before the most stressful days of work, so that the morale of the office does not suffer.

On a daily basis, your EQ will help you be more proactive while guiding the movements of your office to prevent conflicts. For example, if you visualize any disputes coming up during a meeting, you can always use your position as a boss to change the tone of the conversation and ensure that it happens respectably. As the boss, you have the ability and the privilege to look at the larger goals of your team even when they become distracted by minor conflicts. This is a very powerful insight to have since you can inspire your employees to keep working in the right direction while making sure that they don't feel ignored or left out.

The Importance of EQ

As discussed in this chapter, the concept of EQ will radically change your leadership style and your life for the better. It is very important not to stick to rigid ways and outdated methods and to change with the needs of the times. A lower level of EQ can turn into the most challenging hurdle to your growth as a leader, regardless of how skilled or qualified you are.

Instead of always projecting power and being astute, you can come across as a boss who is also a mentor and truly cares about his employees. You must dedicate yourself to the cause of becoming more emotionally aware, and focus your energy in that direction. It will not suffice to keep adding to your analytical skills and your logical reasoning if you cannot back it up with a remarkable set of social skills. By becoming more present in your role as a leader, you will project a kind of confidence that immediately puts your employees at ease. Instead of always worrying about your weaknesses, you can use emotional awareness as a tool to play to your strengths and ensure that you are the best boss that you can be.

CHAPTER 5
THE SECRET SUPERPOWER OF A LEADER

I f you have consciously accepted your role as an emotionally intelligent leader, you will need to learn about one of the most important foundations of Emotional Quotient – vulnerability. Vulnerability is a very conflicting topic to discuss, and it is essential to first dispel the many myths around it before considering how vulnerability can make you the strongest possible version of a leader that you can be. Based on your attitude, the vulnerability can become a superpower, and the journey of opening up your emotions and feelings can leave you completely changed as a person and leader, always for the better.

Conventional wisdom often instantly links vulnerability to weakness, arguing that being highly emotional as a leader makes it easier for other people to manipulate you. There was also a common understanding that any display of vulnerability in a workplace meant that the leader did not have adequate control over the office and lacked a natural leadership quality. As the discussion around emotionally intelligent leaders widens, vulnerability has made a return as a new buzzword as a critical aspect of emotionality. However, it struggles to shed the stigma that it carried with itself in earlier times.

The direct result of this stigma is that individuals often resist embodying vulnerability, especially in the workplace. The cultural trend is that it is best to suppress your vulnerability and be as detached and impersonal as possible while conducting yourself at work. Since we live and work in very competitive times, being vulnerable is equated to being naïve and open to exploitation. People in positions of leadership especially feel the burden of presenting an unfaltering image to their employees because they think that an emotionally infallible leader is more reassuring to workers. This cycle of denying vulnerability actively hinders the creation of an emotionally intelligent work culture.

The perpetuation of this stigma has largely been fear-based. The influence of fear is strong and doesn't always bow down to rational arguments. Hence, the stories that people consume of vulnerability being the cause of failure at work often scare them into rejecting vulnerability, even if they have to turn a blind eye to their subjective position and work environment. The common belief that vulnerable people are most likely to get hurt also reigns among people. Therefore, it is not just a fear of failure but also a very primal fear of pain, which prevents the shedding of the stigma around vulnerability.

It would be false to say that these fears don't have any truth to them. They emerge from the lived experiences of people, and we must accept that people who leave themselves vulnerable also open up a whole new avenue of possible mistreatment. However, what common perceptions ignore is that being vulnerable also means that you are not shutting yourself off to a huge part of your emotional life, and tapping into your truth.

The denial of vulnerability ultimately means the rejection of your most real truth, and the energy that is taken up in suppressing it is immense. In this sense, denying your vulnerability exposes you to the harm of having your cover fall apart. Exploring your vulnerability allows you to both experience and present your truth in a way that leaves you with nothing to hide. In a work environment, especially in the position of leadership, this can be an invaluable quality that makes you different from traditional leaders. Being unafraid of your weakest points means that you don't always have to guard them alone, but that you can discuss them without hesitation and share the burden of resolving them with your team.

VULNERABILITY – WHAT IS IT?

Vulnerability is commonly defined as: 'quality or state of being exposed to the possibility of being attacked or harmed, either physically or emotionally.' It means the state of being open to influence and manipulation by other people. However, in the more emotionally aware age, there have been efforts to redefine vulnerability in a more positive light. In her popular Ted Talk called *The Power of Vulnerability*, the researcher and storyteller, Brene Brown, says that "vulnerability is the core, the heart, the center, of meaningful human experiences."

In giving this definition, she provides a valuable argument against becoming deaf to your vulnerability, as it is the easiest way to drain the meaning from your experiences. The sum of everything that we do and everything that happens to us is located in how we feel about these things. It is central to the human experience that we adequately receive, and process the many situations that life puts us in. Vulnerability is not just a state of being; it's an important approach to a life demanding that you engage with your surroundings and allow them to shape you, instead of becoming rigid in your ways.

COMMON MYTHS AROUND VULNERABILITY

There are many common myths about a vulnerability that can easily be debunked if they are thought through.

Vulnerability is Always Equal to Weakness: As mentioned earlier, this is one of the most common reasons why people are resistant to embodying vulnerability. We live in a culture, which pressurizes us always to be worried about how others perceive us. Due to this, we are told to shut off our emotions and be less honest about how things affect us. However, it can be argued that being detached from your feelings also does not allow you to experience the best emotions that life has to offer like happiness, belonging, courage, love, and contentment. Far from being a permanent weakness, vulnerability is how we gain the strength to truly live.

. . .

Not Everyone Experiences Vulnerability: One of the biggest problems of an emotionally closed culture is that we are made to believe that we are alone in our emotional journeys. We present a face to the people around us, which in turn makes us feel like everyone around us is always collected and detached. This is a lie since every human being goes through many emotional states; some do it more privately while others are more open about it. Emotional vulnerability is one of the universal experiences that unite us as humans.

Being Vulnerable Means Being an Open Book: Vulnerability is not about sharing every little thought or every experience you have had with everyone around you all the time. Being vulnerable does not mean that you can keep no part of your personal life to yourself. It has more to do with trust and with feeling comfortable in presenting the negative aspects of yourself to the world, not just the positive ones.

There are other myths in the same tone as the three that have been elaborated above, but they can be debunked by remembering that vulnerability is universal, it is acceptable, and it is essential. People who continue to believe in the myths about vulnerability do not fare well in the roles of leadership. They can only attain a limited amount of success, no matter how hard they try. Such leaders will find it challenging to keep their workers motivated and together during difficult times. They will also experience higher levels of stress in their leader-role since they choose to remain secretive about their problems. On the other hand, vulnerable people and leaders enjoy the trust of the people around them.

No one can come forward and say that these myths are based on no truth whatsoever, but the opposite assertion is equally true. Vulnerability does require you to be more trusting of other people; however, that is not just so that you may put yourself in harm's way, but so that you may dive into an exercise of openness. The fundamental truth about life is that it is a mixture of happiness and pain. Anyone who tries to avoid the more difficult parts of it inevitably ends up obstructing their own journey toward happiness.

HABITS OF SUCCESSFULLY VULNERABLE PEOPLE

People who successfully become comfortable with their vulnerability share some common traits that are incredibly advantageous to them in both life and leadership. For them, vulnerability is extremely empowering and shows certain strengths of character because they are willing to take risks. Psychoanalyst Robert Stolorow, in his book *Trauma and Human Existence*, highlights some of these traits, to show how our cultural shame around vulnerability is nothing but a poorly informed reaction.

Open to New Experiences: No one can ever predict the outcomes of everything. Most out, our journey through life involves doing things that we are unsure of and putting ourselves in situations that we cannot always control. Vulnerable people keep themselves open to the idea of new experiences. This is not always about big, risky things like moving to a completely new place, but it is also about something as small as trying a hobby that you've always wanted to try. They chase new experiences over material possessions, which gives them a more authentic sense of happiness in life.

Accepting Negative Emotions: While there is an excitement associated with the unpredictability of life, there is also immense anxiety. It is common to have a fear of the unknown, yet vulnerable people do not use that as an excuse not to try new things. With everything that we do, there are always rewards and risks associated, and many times the most fulfilling things are also the most potentially anxiety-inducing for us. Instead of running away from negative feelings of anxiety, they use their vulnerability as the courage to face life's challenges. It doesn't need to be the emotion of anxiety; accepting every negative feeling is the right way to handle them.

. . .

Being Honest About the Bad Things: Another important aspect of not running away from your negative thoughts is accepting that life is a mixed bag of surprises. It is never linear and never devoid of sadness. All human beings experience it in different forms; suffering, illness, loss, trauma, injury, and we all live in the constant fear of our death. Being vulnerable means that we accept that there are some things that we will never be able to change in our lives, yet we don't have to define our whole existence according to them.

Valuing Emotional Intimacy: We may live a life of many social and personal obligations, but for many people, human relationships start feeling burdensome and meaningless because there is no authentic emotional bonding in them. Repressing your emotions is most harmful to how much you can offer to people who depend on you, and it destroys the intimacy in relationships. On the other hand, vulnerable people enter into deep and trusting relationships with people who can reciprocate their values and return their level of emotional commitment. Hence, they often have very fulfilling relationships and friendships that feel natural and free.

Connecting with Strangers: At the core of being vulnerable is being comfortable with putting yourself out there. This means that you do not shy away from the idea of presenting your most authentic self to other people while also expecting and seeing the best in other humans. Vulnerable people find it easy to establish pleasant, honest relationships with people in very minimal ways – smiling at a passerby, or striking up a conversation while waiting in line. Studies suggest that people mostly appreciate behavior like this since it makes them feel a sense of social connection and shared happiness.

. . .

Being a Good Leader: People in positions of management and leadership are under the most pressure to present a collected and calm image all the time. However, with being excessively emotionally detached, there is always the risk of coming across as not human, which discourages true loyalties from forming. Employees feel closer to emotionally vulnerable leaders because they view them as human, just like themselves. This makes them more likely to contribute more honestly to their work and to be more open with their feedback. A more open management style is the best for a healthy collaborative environment where hierarchies do not come in the way of a general level of happiness and productivity.

Kindness to Yourself: The quality of being vulnerable is not only an external quality that is extended to other people. It is, first and foremost, an act of acceptance of one's own self. Vulnerable people accept that they need joy and comfort and that they are not numb to the different ways that life treats them. They try to create an environment for themselves where they can experience happiness in the most unselfish way. They allow themselves to feel gratitude and love while not shaming themselves from having bad moments.

Embracing Vulnerability: Lastly, vulnerability is about embracing the idea of vulnerability itself and making it central to your progress in life. For vulnerable people, all their creativity, joy, and enthusiasm flow from a place of emotional openness, and therefore they are always committed to whatever they do. These people are not afraid of things not turning out how they expected them to, and find a lot of joy in the surprises of life. When they experience negative emotions, they don't hide away from the world until they feel numb, but instead, confess their emotions to themselves and the world.

VULNERABILITY AND LEADERSHIP

Once you have understood that vulnerability is not a weakness, you can explore the many ways in which it makes you a better leader. As detailed in the earlier chapter, the new workforce comprising of emotionally intelligent adults, does not respond well to aggression and crude power. These individuals perform their best work when they feel like they are working in a welcoming environment where their leader is someone who can always be looked up to for guidance, help, and support. They do not just want a boss who will issue orders and evaluate their work with no human connection.

Vulnerability in a leader is perceived as a sign of courage and confidence. You will come across as a person unafraid of his authentic self. You will appear more honest and humane to your employees, which will make them feel like they are equal to you. This equalizing effect of vulnerability is crucial to developing good. It takes a lot of work to maintain an image of perfection, and such an image can easily fall apart at the slightest pressure.

If you make your employees believe that you are perfect and infallible, then you will immediately lose their trust and respect at the first sign of distress from you. With the kind of high-stress situations that you will be confronted to deal with as a leader, you cannot expect that you will always have everything under control. If you are okay with admitting that you don't always have all the answers, then you will be giving legitimacy to the spirit of team effort and empowering your workers to think of independent and creative ways to make things easier for everyone.

Employees who work under vulnerable leaders also feel the most growth in their personal skills and emotional intelligence because they get the opportunity to present their individual voice to someone who is truly willing to listen. They are not constantly made to feel inferior; instead, they feel like they are an indispensable part of a group effort. The right balance between expectation pressure and positive reinforcement achieves the best performance from employees.

As Howard Schultz says, 'you have to be honest and authentic and not hide. I think the leader today has to demonstrate both transparency and vulnerability, and with that comes truthfulness and humility.' The humility that Schultz is talking about is also an important internal check upon your ego, which will enable you to have more authentic evaluations of your performance. You will find yourself growing more as a leader. The best part about adopting vulnerability as a leadership tactic is that it requires no formal training or skill. It is the simplest way you can change yourself. By being honest with yourself and other employees, you will alleviate a lot of anxieties that people have about working in a high-pressure job under a qualified leader.

THE FOUR PRINCIPLES OF VULNERABLE LEADERSHIP

While everyone has a particular kind of vulnerability, there are a few crucial areas of focus where you can channel your vulnerability to strengthen your leadership and help your employees become a team.

Be Visible: First and foremost, you need to show your employees that no amount of adversity will make you hide from them. Be as visible as possible; show up for the most stressful, uncomfortable conversations, and don't be afraid to share emotional space with your co-workers. Let them see your authentic passion for your work. This kind of energy is contagious. If your employees can see how meaningful your work is to you, they will make a greater effort to make their roles meaningful. If they know that you have an emotional stake in your job, they will work harder. You have to set a precedent of having difficult conversations in the most open and sensitive ways. Your employees will pick up on this tendency and be more comfortable and forthcoming with each other.

Trusting Others: Trust is what makes any collaborative space work. It is a complicated concept, but it simply means an attitude of not being overly suspicious and skeptical of those working around you. By building an atmosphere of trust, you will empower many essential qualities. To do so, you have to discuss trust in the workplace. Set your own boundaries and encourage other people to respect each other's boundaries while sharing a workspace. Be clear about how much work you can manage and how much effort you are willing to put into anything.

Over-estimating your ability to contribute to something will lead to inevitable disappointment. Be accountable for your own mistakes while also holding other people accountable to theirs. Discourage gossiping or negative comments about any individual, and do not share any information that is not yours to share. Try to be as non-judgmental as possible. Be generous to your employees whenever you can, and extend them the benefit of the doubt to show them that you place trust in them.

Show Resilience: One of the biggest fears around vulnerability is the risk of failure. Being open and courageous increases your chances of facing difficulties and hurdles, even as it increases the long-term payoffs that you will receive. Make failure a part of your work ethic. Do not shroud it in shame and hide it from your employees, make a point to show your employees that no matter how dejected circumstances are, you have the backbone to rise and finish a task. You have to show that you care about your own effort and the effort of your team above and beyond superficial things like the negative comments of other people and a few instances of getting bad results.

Remember Your Values: Every organization has some values at its core that keep it together. However, as time progresses, it becomes easy to lose sight of these values and become fully immersed in the game of profits and losses. As a vulnerable leader, you have to embody the goals of the company and always be a reminder of why people do their jobs in the first place. Don't just make empty words out of your values – like honesty, trust, integrity, dedication. Transform all of them into observable behaviors. Your employees should be able to say that you possess all the qualities that you demand from them. These values should be a big reserve of assurance and strength to which any team member can come back whenever they feel lost or discouraged in their role.

HOW DOES VULNERABILITY HELP?

If you can effectively bring these four principles to the board, you will master the art of being a vulnerable leader. You will immediately notice a difference in the general attitude of the office as people become more light-hearted. There will be a reduction in stress, and you will find yourself being approached by employees for feedback and help. You will also enjoy a free flow of conversation with them and discover their unique talents and skills.

When you are open and expressive about your desires and fears, you allow the space for help to arrive. If you frankly express your worries to your employees, maybe a member of your team will have faced the same fear and will resonate with you because of it. Perhaps another member will give you suggestions on how to get over that fear. You will not only help yourself; you will also help your team members feel like they have the ability to connect with their leader. Remember, we are all emotional creatures, after all.

Co-workers who go through stressful times tend to bond better over time. Being emotionally vulnerable has the same effect because you let your employees know that they are not just useful to you as employees but important to you as people. If your team understands your drives, your motivations, and the authentic truth behind your goals, they will be able to support your ambition better. People who feel like their work is mere drudgery with no meaning are likely to disengage from their job and not respond at all to the effort of team building. Allow your employees the space for letting their emotions go and let them know that you will be available to address any fears that may prop up in their minds.

EIGHT RESULTS VULNERABLE LEADERS ACHIEVE

Decreasing Tension: Many leaders believe that they can work their way around uncomfortable situations and bury them even though they need to be addressed. That's a fatal flaw in leadership. Vulnerable leaders step up to the task of leasing a difficult discussion and making it normal to talk things out on a human level. This decreases the stress that employees feel while bringing up an important yet uncomfortable topic. It also makes it easier for criticism to flow in a way that employees don't find derogatory or belittling. Vulnerable leaders can significantly reduce stress in their office.

Boosting the Flow of Ideas: Leaders who accept that they don't have all the solutions take a step back from the decision-making role and open up a whole new space for the talents of their team to shine. Therefore, employees feel like they need to give inputs that will stimulate their creative brains and encourage them to always look for new angles to their work. More importantly, if you lead the way by making it normal to try new things even at the cost of failing, you are likelier to have the most innovative ideas flowing around in your office.

Unhindered Communication: A leader has a huge role in deciding the boundaries of his office. He can determine what is acceptable and not acceptable within the working environment. If you, as the leader, can set the example of open, honest conversations, you will set the tone of communication in your office. Team members will share more effectively with each other, and you will reduce your burden of supervising every conversation. This is great for the overall maturity of your office environment, and also helps to build trust among your team members.

Mitigating Problems: Leaders who show a negative response to criticism and bad news, often end up in a situation where their workers are afraid of coming to them with any upsetting information.

This leads to a piling up of the problem until it becomes big enough for the leader to notice. You can easily avoid this by encouraging people to come to you as much as possible with their doubts and concerns. While this will require more effort from you, you will be able to spot and nip many problems in the bud, as opposed to finding these problems later when they are more challenging to resolve.

A Cooperative Environment: Astute and detached leaders can set a trend by which employees pit themselves against each other to gain the favor of their boss individually. While some amount of competition is healthy, without a vulnerable leader guiding it, it can soon become an obstruction to actual work. Employees may try to sabotage each other's work and prevent important information from flowing around to gain an advantage over others. Vulnerable and emotionally intelligent leaders can remove this toxic competitive spirit from their employees because they do not only notice the results that their employees give them, but their overall effort and dedication.

Creating a Fun Workspace: Any workplace, which harbors a lot of secrets, is not a healthy one. People feel like they always have to stay on guard and only interact with their co-workers when necessary. A vulnerable leader encourages people to come forward with all honesty and creates a level of emotional ground for people to interact in. Such a leader can greatly improve the mood of the work environment and cause a fun atmosphere where people can trade jokes and stories without feeling like they will be judged. The younger part of the workforce will especially respond well to such a friendly atmosphere.

Greater Employee Retention: Employees who form an emotional connection with their leaders, their co-workers, and their organization are statistically less likely to abandon the company if things get difficult. They are also less likely to be tempted by offers of more benefits or higher pay if they feel like they exist in an irreplaceable emotional environment. An open leader can make employees become truly attached to the role that they play for their team. They create employees who view their job not just as another opportunity to earn money, but as something that adds meaning to their life. Such employees are invaluable to organizations.

Having Faith: Above all else, you have to have some faith in the very act of being vulnerable. While it might be a terrifying prospect to be open to other people, especially when you are in the position of a leader, you will soon start to notice the positive effects that it has on people. You do not come across as weak by being vulnerable. Other people will see the courage and strength it takes to be honest and admire you for it. They will try to emulate this courage and strongly support you in whatever you undertake. Employees will face difficult situations with you with less fear. This is exactly the kind of feeling you want to inspire in your worker.

When they look at you, they should see the best version of a company-worker that is possible, someone who embodies skill and talent alongside a welcoming and kind personality. You will reduce the number of superficial problems that come up in a workplace and direct everyone's attention to the main task of achieving a common goal. You will also feel more fulfilled since you are letting yourself experience what it is like to risk something to be a better leader.

The feedback and appreciation that you receive from your employees will be genuine. This will make you more assured in your role as a leader. The cycle of mutual encouragement and patience that you set off by being a vulnerable leader will have positive impacts beyond your immediate work environment. It will positively affect the career paths of all your workers, and they will be all the more closely attached to you and your company because of it. This is how successful leaders build loyal workforces that help them reach new heights of success.

CHAPTER 6
WHY A LEADER NEVER ASKS 'HOW'

After reading the first five chapters, you have come a long way in the journey of reshaping your idea of what the best boss is and how to be one. You have been introduced to many radical new ideas that have probably given you a new outlook on your leadership. If you find yourself questioning a lot of your older beliefs, then it is a sign that you have taken the lessons from the earlier chapters well. Any kind of radical self-improvement requires a lot of introspection, and it is only natural that you find your old self-giving away to new, more relevant principles.

By accepting the importance of being emotionally aware and vulnerable, you have taken an enormous step forward in your journey toward becoming a better leader. Being a boss is a lot of power, and it is important not to let it get to your head. You will be truly powerful only once you realize that you cannot force your bossiness onto people and expect any genuine dedication or admiration from them. You need to make them feel as free and comfortable as possible, and only then will you be able to lead them confidently.

Now that you know exactly how to go about transforming your employees into a team, it is time to understand the last aspect of amazing leadership – setting your employees free upon their tasks.

This is yet another new approach that completely differs from traditional methods. It is all about reducing your interference into other people's jobs to a necessary minimum and opening up as much space as possible for your workers to bring their own style and their own sense of responsibility to their tasks. In this chapter, you will learn the importance of being a flexible leader.

HOW MUCH CONTROL IS TOO MUCH CONTROL?

Everyone appreciates a boss who knows what he is doing. Such a boss can inspire confidence in his employees and give them the guidance that they might need on a day-to-day basis. However, it is the worst kind of boss who tries to inject his own knowledge and his own methods into every little task that is assigned to his employees. These bosses attempt to control every tiny aspect of their work and believe that their way is better than everyone else's. This behavior is part of 'micromanagement,' which was elaborated in an earlier chapter.

Micromanagement is a very controlling management style in which someone tries to personally supervise and control every part of a team – its tasks, its people, its mood, and its decisions. This kind of hyper-controlling technique is only effective in very basic, small-scale projects where the manager does not have a larger goal to cater to. However, as a general leadership style, micromanagement can harm company morale. Most micromanagers share the common trait that they do not feel okay with delegating work. Even when they do delegate work, they immediately take it over themselves if they spot any mistakes with how the work is being carried out. They are overly obsessed with small, sometimes insignificant details and do not look at the big picture. Such people spend most of their management time, supervising others, and do it in a very monotonous style. They do not know how to incorporate feedback and other people's opinions. They always require updates on progress at every little stage to the point of hindering other people's work. While these traits are not inherently bad while handling micro situations, you definitely want to avoid them if you are trying to be the best boss.

. . .

The Worst Kind of Boss: Think back on your career and try to list out the worst leaders that you have worked under. Some of these leaders may have been inept at their jobs due to a lack of knowledge or qualifications. However, if they displayed the right attitude, it's likely that they were still able to do their job better than the boss who would keep you under their nose every step of the way. This boss was probably an overbearing figure who people wanted to avoid interacting with at all costs. You must have felt discouraged ever to approach this kind of a leader for help or advice because that would mean that he would take over the whole task for you.

The work you did under that boss probably felt like the most unsatisfying work you have done, and there is also a high chance that your self-esteem took a blow after working with such a leader. Remember, anyone can acquire any related training skills with adequate effort, but the art of being a relaxed boss is something that only a few people can master. Yet, if you can understand the logic behind why absolute control is a destructive concept, then you will find yourself naturally embracing a more flexible leadership style. Just keep in mind that being a controlling person is not so much a leadership style as it is a personality trait, and if you need to improve that aspect of yourself, it will require a profound look into your own beliefs.

Embrace the Loss of Control: The first step toward eroding your need to micromanage is an internal one. Remember two important things. Firstly, there is no way that you will ever know how exactly things are going to turn out. You are only human and have a limited view of things. As you may know from experience, life tends to throw surprises at you without warning, so a large part of living is just adjusting yourself to unpredictable things. Unpredictability will also form a large part of your job as a leader since you are working with so many different people. You can be disciplined in your routine and true to your values, but you will still not be able to avoid unforeseeable situations. It is normal not to be able to visualize exactly how things are going to pan out on a given day.

Secondly, there is no way in which you can fully control something from the beginning to the end. If one individual could see a whole project alone, then we wouldn't need elaborate organizational setups to do any work. Your knowledge, your training, and your experience contribute to making you the best leader you can be, they are not tools for you trying to make everything fall into place in a certain way. Even if you try, it will be an impossible task. This is not your limitation as a leader; it is simply a truth about life and work, which you need to make peace with.

Only when you can completely accept that some loss of control is a natural part of your job will you slowly realize how futile it is to fixate on the 'how.' The more time you spend worrying about the little details that are not working out the way you expected them to, the less time you will have to think about how new and unexpected approaches sometimes make your job easier and more fun.

Efficiency vs. Burnout: This may be a hard pill to swallow, but it is an imperative one. There is a very thin line between being efficient and being so technical that you become inefficient. Take some time to understand this complexity. Not everyone who works under you comes from the same experience and work ethic that you do. There are innovations in education and training every day, and a lot of your subordinates likely have a completely different approach to work than you do.

In such a scenario, if you try to make them copy what you want them to do, exactly how you want them to do it, instead of making them more productive, you will be cramping their natural style. They will possibly find your methods obsolete and feel like they are not getting good results with them. Your employees will hesitate to suggest interesting alternatives to you and continue to try to make your obsessive management style work because they fear that they will be reprimanded. Hence, you will condemn your workers into working with tools that they neither understand nor like. Getting caught in that rut can completely sabotage the trajectory of your growth. Since you already have a good understanding of the importance of being emotionally intelligent, you can notice how this kind of hyper attentiveness to detail can emotionally exhaust many of your employees.

WHY FEAR THE UNEXPECTED?

Look back on your life so far and carefully think about all the good things that have come to you. Visualize all the decisions and roads that led you to the best things in your life – your job, your home, your family, your relationships, etc. You will immediately notice that, for the most part, you did not know what was coming at you. You reached some important milestones while having no control whatsoever over your circumstances.

It is also likely that sometimes things happened in the complete opposite way of how you had planned them, yet they turned out well for you. This is what we mean when we say that absolute control is simply impossible for a human being, and a leader is no different. It is only within our power to make the best out of whatever we are given. Instead of fixating on things not going our way, it is better that we focus on the positives of every situation, and try to fix the negatives as much as we can. Our loss of control over our own lives is not a painful human limitation; it is the very core of our humanity.

It must be admitted, however, that it is equally human to worry about the things that we can't control. After all, we desire our own wellbeing and the wellbeing of those around us. It is hard to make peace with the fact that no matter how careful we are, there is a chance that our loved ones will suffer, that we will suffer, or that we will cause pain to other people. If you are a compassionate person, it is only natural that you find yourself worrying about all the cruel things in the world that you cannot change. However, continually obsessing about something that you cannot change is only going to lead to a quick deterioration of your mental health.

If your focus is not on how you live your life or work toward your goal, but on all the little things that lie outside your control, you will always feel stressed. This stress does add nothing to your life. It does not give you the skills to face challenges, it does not make you a stronger person, and it does not inspire those around you. It is just a black cloud that follows you around. Be careful to create boundaries for yourself when it comes to how much you are willing to worry about something before it becomes a purely negative instinct for you and those around you.

The Alternative: Instead of deciding between worrying and not worrying, there is an alternative approach you can consider to deal with the unexpectedness of life. Once you accept the truth about control, you can simply choose to relax and detach yourself from it. This means that even when you worry about something, you no longer try to change it by exerting control over it or try to use your power to suppress it. Instead, you consciously take a step back, zoom out and look at the bigger picture. How does this new thing affect your plan? Does it make it better? Does it make it worse? What can you realistically do to make this new thing a part of your vision? What is this new thing trying to teach you? By asking yourself questions like these instead of just freaking out because you have lost control, you will gain immense peace of mind.

At work, this translates into dealing with employees who bring their own unique ideas and styles to the table. It also means dealing with any unexpected conditions that come up – both positive and negative ones. Don't be an immovable block of rigid belief; open yourself up to the possibilities that every new occurrence brings. You will find yourself being more focused and creative than ever if you do this. You can become your own worst enemy if you turn a blind eye to all the potential that exists in the adversity around you. If you stay true to your goal more than to your methods, you will discover new paths leading to the same destination every day. You cannot be a true leader if you are not open to the educational potential of every moment.

Liberating Yourself as a Leader: To let go of the things that you cannot change will give you incredible peace as a human being. As a leader, it is the most liberating thing that you can do to your leadership style.

This means that you embrace your role as your employees' guide and start focusing on the 'what' and the 'why' more than the 'how'. You will attain great flexibility in your leadership style once you make this change, and it will yield many positive results. Most importantly, you will genuinely feel freer. You will not be constantly burdened with unnecessary pressure and can direct all your energy to get more positive work done than ever. A leader who appears free and confident is the most trustworthy. This is the sort of leader who truly makes an impression on his co-workers, and takes on every challenge with them. That's the last and most important step in becoming the best boss.

UNDERSTANDING THE WHAT

Behind every project that you will ever lead, there is always going to be a bigger goal that your company is trying to accomplish. All work that happens in an organization has a bigger role to play in the overall trajectory. This is the 'what' of your job. Not only do you need to have a very clear idea of what your situation is, but you also need to be able to strongly project that to your employees and make them realize what the purpose of their individual roles are. You cannot let your employees lose interest in their jobs because they feel like they are not contributing enough to an end goal. Even when the larger end goal is not visible, let them know what your vision is and how they always help fulfilling it. If your subordinates feel like you have a clear idea of where a project is headed, they will have less self-doubt and less hesitation in putting work into it selflessly. By understanding the 'what' you can prevent your workers from feeling lost.

The 'what' is unique to every job, but you can arrive at it by asking yourself two major questions at every stage of progress -

What are the goals I wish to accomplish?: Your goal is not the same as your annual target; it is not the statistical milestones you would like to achieve. Although that target also is important, your personal goal is something that is entirely unique to you and is borne out of the concept that you have for yourself. Attention, don't confuse it with the vision the company thrives for; we will discuss this one later. Your goal should be consistent with the reason for which you have taken the role of a leader. It may mean becoming an emotionally intelligent leader; it may mean changing some key aspects of how your employees work. It may even mean implementing new communication strategies around the office or trying to be less engaged with your work and more engaged in making your employees feel happy.

You must have a clear conception of your own goal above and beyond the target that you are required to meet. By doing so, you will imbue everything that you do, every order that you issue, and every feedback that you give with a larger meaning that corresponds to what you are trying to achieve. Having this sense of a target will provide you with a clear perspective on your work and will make it easy for you to take high stakes decisions. Sometimes you will be in a position where you will need to give up immediate gains to achieve your larger goal. For example, you cannot make your employees work overtime frequently even if that means getting more work done because somewhere down the line, they will face burnout. If your goal is to ensure the overall health and satisfaction of your workers, then you will give them adequate time to take breaks and replenish their energy before coming back to work.

What is my purpose as a leader?: Your purpose as a leader is your own definition of your position. There are a few expectations that your organization and your employees will place upon you, and you must do your best to meet them. At the same time, however, you should be able to tell when you are straying from your values and your purpose. If you have decided that you want to be the best guide that your employees have ever had, then you will have no hesitation whatsoever in implementing certain communication strategies, which makes it easier for them to approach you.

If your purpose is to pull people out of a plateau of productivity, then you will have to be innovative about how things are carried out around the office. The bottom line is that you need first to know what defines your individual style of leadership and not let logistical details blur that vision for you. If you understand this purpose, you will be a strong leader who is not easily derailed by adversity.

UNDERSTANDING THE WHY

Even after understanding the 'what,' if you don't understand the 'why,' then none of this training will be useful for you. Every boss, every organization, and every project have their unique vision and their personal 'why.' You need to get in touch with your own 'why.'

Your Personal Vision: Think about what drives you to do a job. Why did you dedicate a large part of your life trying to gain the skills that would lead you to the position that you are currently in? Yes, you are trying to earn money to support your life, but is your work just about your income? Somewhere along the way, after a few years of experience, people tend to lose touch with the younger version of themselves, who was always motivated by something more than material gains.

Everyone has a different driving force. Maybe you were trying to support your family and make it easier for your parents to live. Perhaps you were trying to prove that you were capable of being independent and successful on your own. Maybe you were in love with your job and the work that you did. Or you wanted to change the world for the better. Perhaps you loved working with your team so much that every day you would look forward to the new challenges. These are the motivations that launched you into the career that you now have, and while you may have accomplished your youthful goals, it is important never to forget what drove you to work in the first place. This will keep you humble and inspired as you grow older and start taking on more experienced roles. It will also help you empathize with the younger employees who come in sharing similar motivations.

Now think about your current goals. Having attained the stability that you craved as a younger person, what is it that motivates you? It will not be surprising if you realize now that you don't think about bigger motivations anymore. This is what losing sight of your vision means. To be an amazing employee and the best boss possible, you need to think about your personal goals and constantly change them as time goes on. If your younger self wanted to be independent, maybe now you want to spend more time training other employees in your office so that they can learn the knowledge that you have accumulated. Perhaps you want to transform your office into a happier place. Take a step back and evaluate what you truly want to achieve. This is your personal vision.

The Organization's Vision: Regardless of how long you have been at your current job, you definitely understand that there are a few things that set it apart from other organizations. You were attracted by these values and visions or have seen them reflected in the kind of work the company does, which has led you to accept a position of leadership with them. The everyday workings of the office are subject to significant change over time. There will always be new structures, new technologies, new styles of work, and new challenges that an organization has to face and adapt to. You don't need to spend a lot of time worrying about these organic changes. Instead, concern yourself with the vision of the company and allow it to transform your leadership style. You will find that this approach helps you to positively influence your employees and make them realize that the work they do is incredibly meaningful.

The vision of the organization could be to excel in its field, to improve the world, or to benefit a targeted group of people. Keep the vision of your organization in mind, and it will help you make important decisions when dilemmas come up. This is also the best way to create a sense of belonging and to carve out a place for yourself within a company that no one else can fill. The best bosses are the ones who always embody the vision of the organization and allow it to affect their working style deeply.

The Project's Vision: Every task that you and your team work on is not just a bunch of orders and targets that you need to meet. Each project a group hands to a manager is part of its greater goals that contributes to the wellbeing of the company. Remember the vision of your project, and don't let it get lost in the chaos and stress of everyday work. You are a competent leader leading a team of skilled individuals. You need to inspire them to trust their own methods and remind them of their purpose whenever they feel drained. This part of your job is even more important than being a technical guide and expert.

Employees who are very good at the technical part of their jobs will get the opportunity to become your best assets. However, this can only happen if they can also absorb your spirit for your job, and understand that everything you do is part of a larger journey that you are undertaking.

The 'why?' is a large, encompassing concept that includes a lot of subjective and unique motivational factors. The 'why' cannot be found within data or progress reports but reflects in your journey and growth as a leader. This is what I meant earlier by liberating your leadership from the confines of micromanaging. We are not robots who can perform a given task with complete detachment. Everything we do forms a part of our life. Our jobs, which take such a vast amount of our time, therefore deserve the same emotional attention. By focusing on why you will experience a different kind of satisfaction that transcends a completed target or a good review. The goal that you wish to accomplish should always be located within the 'why,' and all the work that you do should be a mere means to reach that bigger goal.

UNDERSTANDING THE HOW

You have spent a lot of time reading about how you need to avoid the 'how' of your work, but what exactly is it? We cannot enumerate all the things that make it up because it differs from job to job. But the 'how' of any job are the tasks that are done to see it through, including the little details that change every day. Whenever a project is given to a manager, he has to bring his technical expertise and his managerial sense to divide the work into stages and then assign smaller tasks to his employees.

The boss also determines the expected result and the deadlines that are to be met. He decides the guidelines to be followed, the times at which progress will be evaluated, and does any other work required out of the specification of his job. While all this is part of the leader's work, this is not the only work that the leader must do.

After doing the basic assigning work, the leader should be careful not to intrude too much into the process that is unleashed. An office is essentially a set of variables that the boss can organize to yield a certain kind of result. However, the boss will never be able to be present for every small logistical decision that is made in the project. The 'how' also includes all the different ways that the subordinates will deal with their portion of the work, how many hours they will dedicate to it, who they will consult and what techniques they will bring. You should have faith in the abilities of the employees and show them that they are accountable for their share of the work. You should not treat any hang-ups in the process as your or your employee's failures, but as logistical issues that can be calmly resolved.

You need to be willing to take a step back and allow things to unfold as they will. Such new circumstances will come up every day, and you cannot afford to obsess about the multiple things that happen with every stage of the project completion. You will be the only one who has a more overall view of the progress. Stay alert to any alarming discrepancies, but let the process be as free and flexible as possible. This will feel like a position of risk, but it is actually your strongest position. By getting too involved in any technical fallacy or one aspect of the process, you will risk losing the crucial overall view that you have. Your effort to control the 'how' will result in you losing the overall control that a leader should have.

BE A GUIDE, NOT A DICTATOR

The best bosses make themselves as available as possible for any specific demands and requests that may prop up over the course of the workday. When someone approaches you for guidance, do not try to take over the whole task but only address the specific problem keeping the individual strengths of the person who has approached you in mind. Give them a gentle push in the right direction and allow them to discover the solution on their own. This is how they will be able to resolve a similar problem if it comes up again.

Beyond this basic guidance, try as much as possible to remove yourself from the path of your subordinates. They are good at working with each other; they have all the channels of communication that they need to discuss their approaches. By not getting in their way, you are empowering them to present the best face that they can offer and prove to you why they are the best ones for their role. After all, all your employees have been chosen because they showed an adequate amount of competence at their job. Give them room to adjust to the demands of every new task, and to flourish using their existing set of techniques.

Above all, the most important benefit of being a non-interfering boss is that you will be able to devote time to where you are truly wanted and needed. A mature, intelligent leader knows how to evaluate which situations need their help and which situations are just manageable obstacles which can turn into the best learning curves for their employees. You need to make sure that your employees really feel the sense of satisfaction after every project is finished because they dedicated their best efforts to it and truly felt involved.

Before we head to the conclusion, Do you mind taking just a few minutes to leave a review? I would like to hear if you found this book useful. You can leave your feedback in the Amazon review section.

It would help me a lot, thank you very much.

CONCLUSION

Now, your concept of leadership has probably undergone a radical transformation. This book intended to give you a very realistic portrayal of what it means to be a leader in this day and age, with both its pros and cons. Organizations no longer work in a time where people have complete faith in hierarchies and respect traditional leadership styles.

If you want to become the best boss, you must let go of the very instinct of bossing people around and adopt a more open, vulnerable approach. By becoming a leader who is always empathetic, present, non-judgmental, and ready to guide, you will form closer bonds with your employees and inspire them to work harder than ever, instead of intimidating them into a corner.

With the way the new generation of young workers is shaping up, it is essential to be a boss they can relate to. You cannot be detached from them. We have discussed various strategies through which you can become more emotionally intelligent and aware of the needs of your employees. It also details the importance of making work feel like fun by giving your workers adequate freedom to operate in. I have explained some of the fatal flaws in the traditional approach to leadership, as well as detailed solutions to them.

In the first two chapters, you were given a detailed explanation of what a boss is, along with the many positives and negatives a leadership position entails. Along with this, we talked about what makes a good boss and how leadership is not just about the title or the authority but is a much more invested role. An important aspect of being a good boss is that you become less of a boss and more of a guide to your employees. You cannot ever stop learning or close yourself to the possibility of being wrong. There is an explanation of why bossy leaders can make their employees more unproductive.

In the next couple of chapters, there was a description of what exactly is it that makes the modern leader so different from traditional ones. The workforce has not remained the same over the last few decades, and the things that drive people to work and make them truly dedicate themselves to a job have changed a lot. This is why a successful leader must understand how to tap into the psyche of the new workforce and become aware of their needs. There is a greater focus on emotional awareness, collaboration, team building, and empathy in the office. The modern leader needs to understand all the techniques that can be used to create an environment in their office, which is the most conducive to all their employees.

The last couple of chapters focus on the emotional core of a successful leader and explore the level of control that a leader should exert to achieve the best results. There is a discussion about the importance of being vulnerable and flexible while staying in touch with the big picture instead of being fixated with smaller logistical details.

Regardless of whether you read this book because you just attained a new managerial position or whether you are trying to better yourself as a boss, you will find that you now have a much more critical view of the position of being a boss. You should approach it with much more care and introspection, and attempt the new techniques that have been introduced in this book.

The one piece of advice that you, as a reader and a potential boss, definitely need to take away from this book is that leadership is not a static role. It is a continually changing position that is filled by the human who occupies it. Leadership is not about fitting yourself into a certain image of a good leader; it is about assessing your individual qualities and making them work. Nothing is better for a leader than to be true to his authentic self and let that energy flow into everything he does.

This also means that every step that you take to become a better boss has to come from an internal, self-reflexive space. In the modern world, the line between who you are as a person and a leader is somewhat blurred. Therefore, all the advice given here is geared toward affecting not just your approach to leadership, but your approach to life as a whole. This is the integrated way in which you need to think about your leadership.

Always remember, the potential to becoming the best boss is locked away within you. The process of unlocking does not have anything to do with completely changing your personality or letting go of the values you had as an employee. It is about learning the best way to use your specific set of skills to make things easier for other people while confronting your flaws and insecurities about leadership. Anyone can become the best boss possible if they dare to change their approach to the concept of leadership itself.

When you are determined to become a great leader, don't forget to review this book. Thanks, and I wish you a successful career as the best boss.

RESOURCES

Belyh, A. (2018, January 1). Leader vs. Boss – The 6 Major Differences. Retrieved from Cleverism website: https://www.cleverism.com/leader-vs-boss/

Berrett-Koehler. (2018, September 11). The Importance of Emotional Intelligence in a Leader. Retrieved from Medium website: https://medium.com/@BKpub/the-importance-of-emotional-intelligence-in-a-leader-d1ffc7fd753c

Brené Brown. (2012). Transcript of "The power of vulnerability." Retrieved from Ted.com website: https://www.ted.com/talks/brene_brown_the_power_of_vulnerability/transcript?language=en

Blog - The Difference Between a Boss and a Leader. (n.d.). Retrieved from www.volarisgroup.com website:https://www.volarisgroup.com/blog/article/the-difference-between-a-boss-and-a-leader

Chamarro-premuzic, T. (2013, May 29). Can You Really Improve Your Emotional Intelligence? Retrieved December 3, 2019, from Harvard

Business Review website: https://hbr.org/2013/05/can-you-really-improve-your-em

Dickson, G. (2016, June 15). 5 Ways Emotional Intelligence Makes a Better Leader. Retrieved from Bonus.ly website: https://blog.bonus.ly/5-ways-emotional-intelligence-makes-a-better-leader

Fannin, K. (2016, August 30). Leader vs Boss: 12 Defining Characteristics of a Leader | Intelivate. Retrieved from Intelivate website: https://www.intelivate.com/team-strategy/boss-vs-leader-image

Gourani, S. (2019, April 25). Leading Multiple Generations In Today's Workforce. Retrieved from Forbes website: https://www.forbes.com/sites/soulaimagourani/2019/04/25/leading-multiple-generations-in-todays-workforce/#39d875794636

Holmes, L. (2017, January 16). 8 Habits Of Actively Vulnerable People. Retrieved from HuffPost website: https://www.huffpost.com/entry/habits-of-vulnerable-people_n_587679d8e4b05b7a465d2713

James, J. (2014, May 5). Forget the What and the How - Motivation Is All About the Why. Retrieved from Life In Charge website: https://lifeincharge.com/forget-what-how-all-about-why/

Kankousky, M. (2015, December). How Emotional Intelligence Can Make You a Better Leader - Insperity. Retrieved from Insperity website: https://www.insperity.com/blog/how-emotional-intelligence-can-make-you-a-better-leader/

Knight, R. (2015, August 21). How to Stop Micromanaging Your Team. Retrieved from Harvard Business Review website: https://hbr.org/2015/08/how-to-stop-micromanaging-your-team

La Phan, L. (2018, November 8). 15 unmistakable qualities of bad managers | kununu Blog. Retrieved from kununu Blog website: https://transparency.kununu.com/unmistakable-qualities-of-bad-managers/

Lebowitz, M. W., Allana Akhtar, Shana. (2020, March 16). 26 signs you have a terrible boss, and how to stop them from crushing your happiness. Retrieved from Business Insider website: https://www.businessinsider.com/signs-you-have-a-bad-boss-2016-2-4

Lewis, G. (2017, October 4). Why Being Vulnerable at Work Can Be Your Biggest Advantage, According to Brené Brown. Retrieved from business.linkedin.com website: https://business.linkedin.com/talent-solutions/blog/talent-connect/2017/why-being-vulnerable-at-work-can-be-your-biggest-advantage-according-to-brene-brown

Mahbub, S. (2017, August 6). Choose the Boss Over the Company. Retrieved from Medium website: https://magazine.vunela.com/choose-the-boss-over-the-company-8ff81b96006a

Marr, B. (2017). 14 Simple Expectations Great Employees Have of Their Boss. Retrieved February 2, 2020, from Linkedin.com website: https://www.linkedin.com/pulse/14-simple-expectations-great-employees-have-boss-bernard-marr/

Mullholand, B. (2018, July 20). Don't Micromanage: How It Destroys Your Team and How to Avoid It | Process Street | Checklist, Workflow and SOP Software. Retrieved from Process Street website: https://www.process.st/micromanage/

Murphy, M. (2017, March 12). The Secret Fear That Causes Bosses To Micromanage. Retrieved from Forbes website: https://www.forbes.com/sites/markmurphy/2017/03/12/the-secret-fear-that-causes-bosses-to-micromanage/#bebbb831b952

Tredgold, G. (2016, December 20). 10 Simple Expectations That Great Teams Have of Their Leaders. Retrieved from Inc.com website: https://www.inc.com/gordon-tredgold/10-simple-things-that-teams-expect-from-their-leader.html

Wolfe, P. (2020, February 22). Managing today's workforce means recognizing generational differences. Retrieved from Crain's Cleveland Business website: https://www.crainscleveland.com/education/managing-todays-workforce-means-recognizing-generational-differences

Printed in Great Britain
by Amazon